STUDY GUIDE FOR
SENSATION AND PERCEPTION

FIFTH EDITION

E. BRUCE GOLDSTEIN
University of Pittsburgh

Brooks/Cole Publishing Company

I**T**P® An International Thomson Publishing Company

Pacific Grove • Albany • Belmont • Bonn • Boston • Cincinnati
Detroit • Johannesburg • London • Madrid • Melbourne • Mexico City
New York • Paris • Singapore • Tokyo • Toronto • Washington

Assistant Editor: *Jennifer Wilkinson*
Marketing Team: *Alicia Barelli, Aaron Eden*
Editorial Assistant: *Rachael Bruckman*
Production Coordinator: *Dorothy Bell*

Cover Design: *Lisa Mirski Devenish, E. Kelly Shoemaker*
Cover Image: *Damir Polić*
Printing and Binding: *Webcom Limited*

For more information, contact:

BROOKS/COLE PUBLISHING COMPANY
511 Forest Lodge Road
Pacific Grove, CA 93950
USA

International Thomson Editores
Seneca 53
Col. Polanco
11560 México, D. F., México

International Thomson Publishing Europe
Berkshire House 168-173
High Holborn
London WC1V 7AA
England

International Thomson Publishing GmbH
Königswinterer Strasse 418
53227 Bonn
Germany

Thomas Nelson Australia
102 Dodds Street
South Melbourne, 3205
Victoria, Australia

International Thomson Publishing Asia
60 Albert Street
#15-01 Albert Complex
Singapore 189969

Nelson Canada
1120 Birchmount Road
Scarborough, Ontario
Canada M1K 5G4

International Thomson Publishing Japan
Hirakawacho Kyowa Building, 3F
2-2-1 Hirakawacho
Chiyoda-ku, Tokyo 102
Japan

Printed in Canada

10 9 8 7 6 5 4 3 2

ISBN 0-534-36250-8

TABLE OF CONTENTS

The following subheadings are included for each of the chapters:

Introductory Statement
Chapter Organization
Table of Contents and Key Terms
Notes
Definitions of Key Terms
Test Yourself

INTRODUCTION

Welcome to the Study Guide to *Sensation & Perception*, 5th edition. The purpose of this study guide is to supplement your textbook, by providing information that will make it easier for you to learn the material in the text.

Your text contains a large number of facts and principles that you need to learn to understand the senses and perception. Your text book and this study guide contain a number of features designed to make this task easier, and to help you go beyond simply learning lists of seemingly unconnected facts about the senses and perception.

A key feature of your text is its organization. The first four chapters are designed to lead you step-by-step through most of the basic principles you will need to know to understand the rest of the material in the book. Especially for those chapters, but often for others as well, one section builds on the next, so it is important that you understand each section before going on to the next one.

This organization is also important because research in learning and memory has shown that material that is presented or studied in an organized manner is much easier to remember than material that is presented or studied as random collections of facts or terms. This means that one of the most effective things you can do in studying the text is to become aware of its organization.

You can use this study guide to help you perceive the way each chapter is organized by reading the brief statement and summary of chapter organization at the beginning of each chapter of the study guide. But being aware of the chapter organization is just a starting point for your studies. Your ultimate goal in reading the text should be to <u>learn the material in the chapter well enough so you can explain each point in the chapter in your own words</u>. I strongly recommend that you do not try to memorize definitions. Use the book definitions as a starting point for creating your own explanations of the terms or principles you want to learn. My experience as a teacher has taught me that I truly understand something only when I have reached the point where I can explain it to someone else.

Here is a step-by-step procedure that you might find helpful in learning the material in each chapter. Since people's learning styles differ, you may want to modify this procedure. Do what works for you, but remember that your goal is to be able to describe the material in the book in your own words, as if you are explaining it to someone else.

1. Become aware of the chapter's organization by checking the summary in this study guide and skimming the main chapter headings in the chapter Table of Contents in this study guide or in the text.

2. Read the chapter or a section of the chapter.

3. Study the material in more depth by mastering small sections at one time. For each section, answer the study questions at the end of the chapter, in your own words. Some people find it helpful to write these answers down, others say them out loud, or "verbalize" them "in their head." Whichever method you use, creating answers by copying word for word from the text is probably not the best way to learn the material. Instead, use the text as a guide to help you make up your own answer.

4. Use the Table of Contents and Key Terms in this study guide to be sure you understand the key terms in the chapter. These terms are listed in order of their appearance and are defined in the Key Terms section for each chapter. (Definitions of the key terms for all of the chapters together also appears in the Glossary at the end of your text.)

5. Check the Notes section of this study guide. This section highlights concepts that are especially important or which some students find difficult to understand. In addition, this section also often contains summary tables. Use these tables as a way to perceive the "big picture" in a section (Looking at these tables may help you to see more clearly how a number of studies are related to each other), and as a way to clarify individual points within each section. (Usually, each "cell" of a table summarizes a main concept or experiment.)

6. After you feel you know the material in a chapter, test yourself by answering the multiple choice questions in this study guide, and answering any other questions that are included in the Test Yourself section. The number in parentheses for each question is the number of

the study question in the text associated with that question. The answers to the questions are at the end of this study guide.

There are no "fill in the blank" or essay questions in the study guide because this way of testing is provided by the study questions at the end of each chapter in the text. Check your knowledge by answering the study questions. Refer back to the book or any answers you may have written down earlier only after you have answered the questions.

This technique of answering the study questions without the help of the book or your notes is an important one, because students often leave out this step, with dire consequences. Students have come into my office after doing poorly on an exam and said "I knew the material," when it is apparent from their exam score and from talking with them that they had studied by simply reading over the material, without taking the crucial step of testing themselves to see if they really knew it. They had created the <u>illusion</u> that they knew the material when in reality they had just read it. There's a big difference between looking over the material and really testing yourself on it, and for some students, this testing step is crucial.

7. If your exams will include multiple choice questions, it may be useful for you to realize that the multiple choice questions on your exam will often be based directly on one of the study questions in your textbook. For example, consider the following study question from Chapter 1 and its associated multiple choice question:

<u>Study Question 18</u>: What is the doctrine of specific nerve energies? Who is associated with it? (This question appears on page 27 of your text)

<u>Multiple Choice Question</u>:

_____ proposed the doctrine of specific nerve energies.
(a) Muller
(b) Kepler
(c) Descartes
(d) Aristotle

In this example, the answer to the multiple choice question comes directly from the second sentence in the study question (The answer is a). Sometimes the link won't be quite so obvious, as in the following example, from Chapter 2.

<u>Study Question 11</u>: How do the rods and cones differ in shape and distribution on the retina? (This question is on page 68 of your text)

<u>Multiple Choice Question:</u>
Cone receptors are found
(a) only in the fovea
(b) only in the peripheral retina
(c) in both the fovea and the peripheral retina
(d) in two of the four layers of the retina.

If you have answered the study question you should know that the answer to the multiple choice question is c. Sometimes more than one study question is relevant to a particular multiple choice question. For example, Study Question 12 (What is the fovea? The peripheral retina? Which area of the retina contains only cones? Where are most of the cones?) contains information you could use to answer the question above. It also is relevant to the following question:

Most of the cones are located in
(a) the peripheral retina
(b) the fovea

When you get to chapter 2, you will find the answer to this question on page 36 of your text.

The purpose of these examples is to emphasize the importance of learning the answers to the study questions. Knowing these answers will help you answer fill in the blank questions, essay questions and multiple choice questions.

8. Finally, a word about highlighters. Many students read textbooks with highlighter-in-hand and create large areas of yellow on each page. I understand why students do this, because when I was a student I also liked to highlight. However, depending only on highlighting to learn the material can be very dangerous, for a number of reasons: (1) Some students highlight almost everything, thereby missing the point of highlighting, which is to emphasize the <u>key points</u> in the chapter; (2) highlighting creates the illusion of active involvement (you are, after

5

all moving your hand as you decide what to highlight), when, in reality, the activity involved is not the kind that will really help you remember what you are reading. The activity that aids memory is the kind of active thinking about what the material means that would be involved in explaining the material to someone else. So my advice is to either avoid highlighting altogether, or, if you feel it helps, don't let highlighting become a substitute for the truly active process of creating your own answers to the study questions.

Good luck in your study of perception. I hope the textbook, in combination with this study guide, makes your learning easier. If you get to a point where you feel you need help in understanding any of the material in the text, or if you have a question about the senses or perception that is not covered in the text, please feel free to email me at bruceg+@pitt.edu and I will do my best to answer your question.

Bruce Goldstein
University of Pittsburgh

TABLES

CHAPTER 1

INTRODUCTION TO PERCEPTION

This chapter expresses one of the main messages of the book: Perception is a <u>process</u> consisting of a number of steps. The existence of this processes testifies to the complexity of perception. But just because perception is a complex process does not mean that the study of perception has to be difficult. The idea behind this book is to present the basic principles behind the process of perception in a step-by-step fashion, starting at a basic level and building towards the understanding of more complex material. For those with no background in biology, all of the basic concepts you will need to understand the material in the text are included in the initial chapters.

CHAPTER ORGANIZATION

1. How the perceptual process can be divided into a sequence of steps. This process can be studied by looking at relationships between the outputs of the various stages.

2. The behavioral approach to perception, including some of the techniques that are used to measure perception behaviorally.

3. The physiological approach to perception, including the basic terms and principles needed to understand the structure of the nervous system and the transmission of nerve impulses.

4. A number of reasons why we are interested in studying perception.

TABLE OF CONTENTS WITH KEY TERMS

Note: Numbers in parentheses indicate page numbers in the textbook.

- difference threshold
- just noticeable difference
- Weber's law

Magnitude Estimation: Measuring Perception Above Threshold
- magnitude estimation
- power functions
- Stevens' power law
- response compression
- response expansion

The Physiological Approach: Linking Stimulation And Neural Firing (13)

The Physiological Approach: Early History

Neurons And Electrical Signals
- doctrine of specific nerve energies
- nerves
- neurons
- cell body
- dendrites
- axon
- nerve fibers
- receptor

Recording Electrical Signals In Neurons
- ion
- microelectrode
- recording electrode
- resting potential
- action potential
- permeability

Basic Properties Of Action Potentials
- propagated response
- all-or-none response
- refractory period
- spontaneous activity

Chemical And Electrical Events At The Synapse
- synapse
- presynaptic neuron
- postsynaptic neuron
- neurotransmitter
- receptor sites

- excitation   - inhibition

Basic Structure Of The Brain
- **cerebral cortex**
- **modular organization**
- **primary receiving area**
- **occipital lobe**
- **temporal lobe**
- **parietal lobe**
- **nuclei**

NOTES: CHAPTER 1

Note: Numbers in parentheses indicate page numbers in the textbook.

Distal and Proximal Stimuli (2)

There are two different kinds of stimuli. There is the <u>stimulus in the environment</u> (distal) and the <u>stimulus actually received by the person's receptors</u> (proximal). We can understand the difference between distal and proximal stimuli by considering John, standing across the room.

To describe John as a <u>distal stimulus</u> we would describe everything there is to describe about John's physical appearance: He is 6 feet tall and weighs 180 points, is wearing brown loafers, gray pants, and a plaid shirt. His hair is brown and close cut, and he has a tattoo on his right bicep. These characteristics, and many more, describe John, and it would take a great deal of description to capture all there is to know about John's appearance.

To describe the <u>proximal stimulus</u> associated with John we would consider only those characteristics of John that actually reach the receptors in the retina. Thus the proximal stimulus would perhaps include portions of his plaid shirt or the fact that he has close-cropped dark hair. But if John is sitting behind a table, his pants would not be imaged on our retina, and since he is wearing his plaid shirt, there is also no retinal image of the tattoo on his arm. Furthermore, if John were to start walking away from us, the distal stimulus would not change, but the proximal stimulus would get smaller on the retina. In this situation, the distal stimulus remains constant, while the proximal stimulus varies depending on what view is present, how close the stimulus us, etc.

Neurons, Excitation and Inhibition (14)

Some students are surprised that the nervous system is a major topic in their perception course. In fact, some students become quite anxious when they realize that the study of perception involves neurons, nerve axons, and synapses. However, the basic principles behind the physiological approach to perception are actually quite simple. For example, nervous system operation can be described, on a simplified level, as follows:

1. Electrical signals are generated in the receptors, by a process called transduction..

2. These electrical signals, called action potentials, are transmitted in cells called neurons.

3. Each neuron connects with many other neurons at a place called the synapse.

4. When the action potential reaches the synapse, the end of the neuron releases neurotransmitter that either excites the next neuron (increases the chances that another action potential will be generated), or inhibits it (decreases the chances that another action potential will be generated).

Of course, the details of each of these steps is more complicated than this. But these four steps provide a starting point upon which to build. Study the material on pages 14-20 of your textbook carefully, paying special attention to study questions 18-27 at the end of the chapter. Learning this material will provide a firm foundation for the further elaboration of the physiological approach in Chapter 2.

KEY TERMS: CHAPTER 1

Absolute threshold. The minimum stimulus energy necessary for an observer to detect a stimulus

Action potential. Rapid increase in positive charge in a nerve fiber that is propagated down the fiber. Also called a nerve impulse.

Adjustment, method of. A psychophysical method in which the experimenter or the observer slowly changes the stimulus until the observer detects the stimulus.

All-or-none response. The nerve impulse either fires or it doesn't. When it does fire, it has just one size no matter what the intensity of the stimulus that generated the response.

Axon. The part of the neuron that conducts nerve impulses over distances. Also called the nerve fiber.

Behavioral approach to perception. The approach that focuses on the relationship between the physical properties of stimuli and the perceptual response. (the stimulus-perception relationship).

Cell body. The part of a neuron that contains the neurons metabolic machinery and that receives stimulation from other neurons.

Cerebral cortex. Thin layer of neurons that covers the surface of the brain, which is responsible for higher functions such as perception and thinking.

Classical psychophysical methods. The methods of limits, adjustment, and constant stimuli, described by Fechner for measuring thresholds.

Constant stimuli, method of. A psychophysical method in which a number of stimuli with different intensities are presented repeatedly in a random order.

Dendrites. Nerve processes on the cell body that receive stimulation from other neurons.

Difference threshold. The minimal detectable difference between two stimuli.

Distal stimulus The stimulus in the environment (usually at a distance from the observer.)

Doctrine of specific nerve energies. A principle stating that the brain receives environmental information from sensory nerves and that the brain distinguishes between the different senses by monitoring the activity in these sensory nerves.

Excitation. A condition that facilitates the generation of nerve impulses.

Excitatory. Referring to the type of neurotransmitter associated with increases in the rate of nerve firing. Can also refer to neural responses that are associated with increases in firing rate.

Excitatory response. The response of a nerve fiber in which the firing A condition that decreases the likelihood that nerve impulses will be generated.

Inhibitory response. The response of a nerve fiber in which the firing rate decreases due to inhibition from another neuron.

Ions. Charged molecules found floating in the water that surrounds nerve fibers.

Just noticeable difference (JND). The smallest difference in intensity that results in a noticeable difference between two stimuli.

Limits, method of. A psychophysical method for measuring the threshold in which the experimenter presents stimuli in alternating ascending and descending series.

Localization of function. The principle that specific areas of the brain serve specific functions.

Magnitude estimation. A psychophysical method in which the subject assigns numbers to a stimulus that are proportional to the subjective magnitude of the stimulus.

Method of adjustment. See Adjustment, method of.

Method of constant stimuli. See Constant stimuli, method of.

Method of limits. See Limits, method of.

Microelectrode. A thin piece of wire or glass that is small enough to record electrical signals from single nerve fibers.

Modular organization. The organization of specific functions into specific brain structures.

Nerve fiber. In most sensory neurons, the long part of the neuron that transmits electrical impulses from one point to another. Also called the axon.

Nerve. A group of nerve fibers traveling together.

Neural processing. Operations that transform electrical signals within a network of neurons, or which transforms the response of individual neurons.

Neuron. A cell in the nervous system that generates and transmits electrical impulses.

Neurotransmitter. A chemical stored in synaptic vesicles that is released in response to a nerve impulse and has an excitatory or inhibitory effect on another neuron.

Nuclei. Small areas in the nervous system at which many synapses occur.

Occipital lobe. A lobe at the back of the cortex that is the site of the cortical receiving area for vision.

Permeability. A property of a membrane that refers to the ability of molecules to pass through the membrane. If the permeability to a molecule is high, the molecule can easily pass through the membrane.

Phenomenological method. Method of determining the relationship between stimuli and perception in which the experimenter asks the subject to describe what he or she perceives.

Physiological approach to perception. As used in this book, this term refers to explanations of perceptual processes based on the relationship between physiological processes and perception. Related to the physiological approach to perception is the study of "pure" physiology, in which physiological processes of sensory systems are studied but are not directly related to perception.

Physiology-perception relationship. The relationship between physiological activity in the nervous system and perception.

Postsynaptic neuron. A neuron on the receiving side of a synapse that receives neurotransmitter from the presynaptic neuron.

Power function. A mathematical function of the form $P = KS^n$, where P is perceived magnitude, K is a constant, S is the stimulus intensity, and n is an exponent.

Presynaptic neuron. A neuron on the sending side of the synapse, which releases neurotransmitter onto the postsynaptic neuron.

Primary receiving area. The area of the cerebral cortex that first receives most of the signals initiated by a sense's receptors.

Propagated response. A response, such as a nerve impulse, that travels all the way down the nerve fiber without decreasing in amplitude.

Proximal stimulus. Stimulus that stimulates the receptors. For example, the image on the retina is a proximal stimulus.

Psychophysics. Methods for quantitatively measuring the relationship between properties of the stimulus and the subject's experience.

Rat-man demonstration. The demonstration in which presentation of a "ratlike" or "manlike" picture influences an observer's perception of a second picture, which can be interpreted either as a rat or as a man.

Receptor sites. Small areas on the postsynaptic neuron that are sensitive to specific neurotransmitters.

Receptor. A sensory receptor is a neuron sensitive to environmental energy that changes this energy into electrical signals in the nervous system.

Recognition. The ability to place an object in a category that gives it meaning. For example, recognizing a particular red object as a tomato.

Recording electrode. A small shaft of metal or glass that, when connected to appropriate electronic equipment, records electrical activity in nerves or nerve fibers.

Refractory period. The time period of about 1/1,000 second that a nerve fiber needs to recover from conducting a nerve impulse. No new nerve impulses can be generated in the fiber until the refractory period is over.

Response compression. The result when doubling the physical intensity of a stimulus less than doubles the subjective magnitude of the stimulus.

Response expansion. The result when doubling the physical intensity of a stimulus more than doubles the subjective magnitude of the stimulus.

Resting potential. The difference in charge between the inside and the outside of the nerve fiber when the fiber is not conducting electrical signals.

Spontaneous activity. Nerve firing that occurs in the absence of environmental stimulation.

Stevens's power law. A law concerning the relationship between the physical intensity of a stimulus and the perception of the subjective magnitude of the stimulus. The law states that $P = KS^n$, where P is perceived magnitude, K is a constant, S is the stimulus intensity, and n is an exponent.

Stimulus-perception relationship. The relationship between physical stimuli in the world and what an organism perceives.

Stimulus-physiology relationship. The relationship between the stimulus and the physiological response to the stimulus.

Synapse. A small space between the end of one neuron and the cell body of another neuron.

Temporal lobe. A lobe on the side of the cortex that is the site of the cortical receiving area for hearing.

Texture gradient. The pattern formed by a regularly textured surface that extends away from

Threshold, absolute. See Absolute threshold.

Threshold, difference. See Difference threshold.

Top-down processing. Processing that starts with the analysis of high-level information, such as the context in which a stimulus is seen.

Weber's law. A law stating that the just noticeable difference (JND) equals a constant (K), called the Weber fraction, times the size of the stimulus (S). This law is usually expressed in the form $K = JND/S$.

TEST YOURSELF

Add the appropriate labels to indicate each of the lobes of the brain. (See Figure 1.23 to check your answer.)

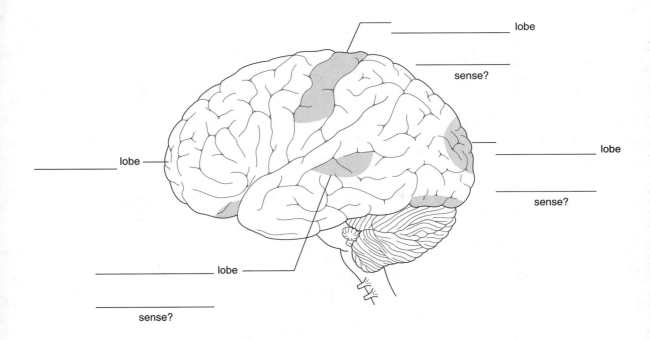

_____ lobe

_____ sense?

_____ lobe

_____ lobe

_____ sense?

_____ lobe

_____ sense?

MULTIPLE-CHOICE QUESTIONS

Numbers in parentheses refer to study questions in the textbook. Answers are at the end of the study guide.

1.1 According to the discussion in Chapter 1, a stage play and perception are similar because both (1)
   a) have casts of characters
   b) have a beginning, middle, and an end
   c) have lead characters and supporting players
   d) have activity that occurs behind the scenes

1.2 Which of the following relationships is most difficult to measure? (5)
a) Stimulus-perception
b) distal stimulus-proximal stimulus
c) physiology-perception
d) stimulus-physiology

1.3 The behavioral approach to perception is concerned with studying the relationship between (6)
a) stimuli and physiological events in the nervous system
b) physiological events and perception
c) stimuli and perception
d) thoughts and perception

1.4 Which of the following is most closely related to the phenomenological method, as discussed in Chapter 1? (7)
a) method of adjustment
b) the rat-man demonstration
c) magnitude estimation
d) free association technique

1.5 In the method of _____ the experimenter presents stimuli in random order. (9)
a) limits
b) adjustment
c) constant stimuli

1.6 If the just noticeable difference for lifting a 600-gram weight is 20 grams, the just noticeable difference for lifting a 3,600-gram weight would be _____ grams (assume the Weber fraction is constant). (10, 11)
a) 40   c) 160
b) 80   d) 360

1.7 If the exponent in the power function which describes the relationship between stimulus intensity and sensation is greater than 1.0 this means that doubling the intensity (13, 15)
a) doubles the sensation
b) increases the sensation but does not double it
c) decreases the sensation
d) more than doubles the sensation

1.8 Aristotle said that the mind was located in the (16)
a) pineal gland
b) heart
c) brain
d) lungs

1.9 The receptor is most closely related to which of the following parts of the neuron? (19)
a) axon
b) dendrites
c) synapse
d) cell body

1.10 Which structure below is responsible for transduction? (20)
a) the receptor
b) dendrites
c) synapse
d) cell body

1.11 Increasing the pressure on a touch receptor will usually influence the _____ of the neuron associated with this receptor. (23)
a) size of the nerve impulse
b) rate of firing

1.12 The steps in the perceptual process always occur in a fixed order, starting with the stimulus and ending with perception.(30)
a) True
b) False

CHAPTER 2

RECEPTORS & NEURAL PROCESSING

Chapter 2 is the first in a series of three chapters that are designed to introduce most of the basic physiological principles that will apply throughout the remainder of the text. These chapters focus on the visual system, but as you will see, the principles we establish in Chapters 2, 3, and 4 will be repeated both in the other chapters on visual perception and in the chapters on hearing, the cutaneous senses, and the chemical senses.

CHAPTER ORGANIZATION

1. The nature of light, the stimulus for vision.

2. The basic structure of the visual system, including the visual pathways, focusing mechanisms, and receptors. In addition, how the action of light on the receptors generates electrical signals.

3. Duplicity theory. This section carries the <u>major message of the chapter: Perception is determined by the structure of our perceptual system</u>. This is accomplished by comparing perception that is determined by the rod receptors to perception that is determined by the cone receptors. As you will see, these receptors differ in a number of ways and these differences can be correlated with differences in perception.

4. Neural processing, created by a combination of excitation, inhibition, and convergence.

5. How neural processing can be applied to understanding (a) receptive fields; (b) differences between rod vision and cone vision, and (c) the effects of lateral inhibition.

TABLE OF CONTENTS AND KEY TERMS

The Rod And Cone Receptors: Shape And Distribution
- **fovea**
- **peripheral retina**
- **pigment epithelium**
- **blind spot**

The Rod And Cone Receptors: Transducing Light Into Electricity
- **visual pigment**
- **opsin**
- **retinal**
- **visual transduction**
- **isomerization**
- **enzyme cascade**

<u>Duplicity Theory: Different Receptors For Different Perceptions</u> (42)
- **duplicity theory of vision**

Dark Adaptation Of The Rods And Cones
- **dark adaptation**
- **dark adaptation curve**
- **dark adapted sensitivity**
- **light adapted sensitivity**
- **rod monochromat**
- **rod-cone break**
- **pigment bleaching**
- **pigment regeneration**

Spectral Sensitivity Of The Rods And Cones
- **monochromatic light**
- **spectral sensitivity**
- **sensitivity**
- **spectral sensitivity curve**
- **rod spectral sensitivity curve**
- **Purkinje shift**
- **absorption spectrum**
- **spectrophotometer**
- **microspectophotometry**
- **short-wavelength pigment**
- **medium-wavelength pigment**
- **long-wavelength pigment**
- **two-color threshold method**

NOTES: CHAPTER 2

Receptors and Perception

 The Table below summarizes some of the properties of the receptors and how these properties correlated with perception

Table 2.1: Relationship between rod and cone pigments and perception

Pigments	Resulting Perception
Absorbing light: Cone and rod pigments absorb light in specific regions of the spectrum. The cones tend to absorb light at longer wavelengths.	Cone spectral sensitivity curve indicates more sensitivity at longer wavelengths than rod spectral sensitivity. Rod spectral sensitivity matches the absorption spectrum of the rod pigment. The shift between rod and cone spectral sensitivity is called the Purkinje shift.
Regeneration: Cone visual pigment regenerates more rapidly than rod visual pigment.	Increase in cone sensitivity during dark adaptation is more rapid than the increase in rod sensitivity.

We can draw similar connections between physiology and perception by focusing on the neural connections of the receptors.

Table 2.2: Relationship between rod and cone wiring and perception (54)

Wiring	Result: Sensitivity	Result: Acuity
Rods converge more than cones (greater spatial summation)	Rod sensitivity is greater than cone sensitivity	Rod acuity is worse than cone acuity

<u>Receptive Fields</u> (51)

The receptive field is one of the most important concepts in sensory physiology. It is important to remember that the receptive field is a property of a <u>single neuron</u>. These single neurons can be anywhere in the visual system (and, as we will see later in the book, these same principles hold for other sensory systems as well). The receptive field of a neuron is the area on the receptor surface that influences firing of a cell. (Later we will modify that definition slightly, but this is a good starting place.). There are a number of important things to remember about receptive fields:

1.   A receptive field is a <u>property</u> of a <u>single neuron</u>. It is not a property of an area on the retina or an area in some other structure.

2.   Receptive fields are not <u>located</u> in the lateral geniculate nucleus or the cortex, or any other structure within the visual system. Receptive fields are located <u>on the receptor surface</u>. (That's why they are called <u>receptive</u> fields!). Thus, there is no such thing as a receptive field in the brain, but we can determine the location <u>on the retina</u> of the receptive field of a single neuron in the brain.

3.   Notice that according to our definition, stimulation of the receptive field "influences," not "increases" the neuron's firing rate. Thus, stimulation of the receptive field can cause either an increase or a decrease in the firing of a neuron. The important thing is that *something* happens. Receptive fields, therefore, often have both excitatory and inhibitory areas.

4.   All of the receptors in a neuron's receptive field are connected to that neuron in some way. The connection is usually not a direct one, but one that travels from the receptors and through many other neurons, before reaching the target neuron.

Effects of Inhibition

Inhibition is an extremely important concept, because it is one of the primary mechanisms responsible for neural processing. Some of the effects of inhibition are

1. Center-surround antagonism. (52) When both the excitatory center and inhibitory surround of a center-surround receptive field are stimulated simultaneously, they have opposite effects and so cancel each other. This also works with inhibitory center, excitatory surround receptive fields.

2. Simultaneous contrast. (57) This is an example of how inhibition can influence perception. Even though the two squares in Figure 2.41 reflect exactly the same amount of light into our eye, the one on the left looks darker, because it receives more inhibition from neurons surrounding it that are stimulated by the higher-intensity surrounding area.

3. Mach bands. (59) This is another example of how inhibition influences perception. Even though the rectangular stripe in Figure 2.45 is the same intensity all the way across its width, you can see dark and light bands near the border. These bands are not really in the stimulus, but are added to your perception by lateral inhibition.

The Difference Between Physical and Perceptual (64)

Both simultaneous contrast and Mach bands are examples of the difference between physical and perceptual. It is extremely important to keep this difference in mind, because we can make the distinction between physical and perceptual for every perceptual phenomenon we will discuss in this book. There is always a physical stimulus and a perceptual response. The reason it is important to distinguish between the physical and perceptual is that they are often not the same, so our perceptions do not always correspond to the physical properties of the stimuli. For example, the two inner squares in Figure 2.41 each reflect the same amount of light (physical), but they appear different (perceptual); each of the rectangular stripes in Figure 2.45a have the same intensity across their width (physical), but we see small bands near the borders (perceptual). Table 2.3 summarizes some examples of situations in which the physical and the perceptual do not match.

Table 2.3: Situations in which physical and perceptual do not match

Phenomenon	Physical Stimulus	Perception
Blind spot (38)	Spot of light is present	Spot vanishes when on blind spot.
Dark adaptation (42-45)	A test light with constant intensity or A light that can't be seen at the beginning of dark adaptation.	Light appears to get brighter as dark adaptation proceeds Light becomes visible as dark adaptation proceeds
Visual acuity (55-56)	A small visual detail	Detail can be seen by cones, but not by rods
Simultaneous contrast (57)	Two identical patches, one surrounded by a dark background, one surrounded by a light background.	The two patches appear different (Figure 2. 41)
Mach bands (59-62)	A bar with the same light intensity across its width	Brightness changes near the border (Mach band) (Figure 2.45)

Table 2.3 (continued)

Phenomenon	Physical Stimulus	Perception
Mach card (62)	A stationary card with constant shading	Card perceptually flips and brightness of the card's sides appears to change.
Surface curvature and brightness (63)	Displays in Figure 2.51 which both have the same intensity distributions	Difference in intensity on left and right sides is less apparent for curved surfaces in 2.51b.
Two-point threshold (64)	The skin is stimulated at two points separated by a small distance	Two points are felt on fingertips, but only one point is felt on the arm.

KEY TERMS: CHAPTER 2

Absorption spectrum. A plot of the amount of light absorbed by a visual pigment versus the wavelength of light.

Accommodation (focus). The eye's ability to bring objects located at different distances into focus by changing the shape of the lens.

Adapting field. A field of light presented to adapt the receptors.

Amacrine cell. A neuron that transmits signals laterally in the retina. Amacrine cells synapse with bipolar cells and ganglion cells.

Bipolar cell. A neuron that is stimulated by the visual receptors and sends electrical signals to the retinal ganglion cells.

Blind spot. The small area where the optic nerve leaves the back of the eye. There are no visual receptors in this area so small images falling directly on the blind spot cannot be seen.

Center-surround antagonism. The competition between the center and surround regions of a center-surround receptive field.

Center-surround receptive field. A receptive field that consists of a roughly circular excitatory area surrounded by an inhibitory area, or a circular inhibitory center surrounded by an excitatory surround.

Cones. Cone-shaped receptors in the retina that are primarily responsible for vision in high levels of illumination, and for color vision and detail vision.

Contralateral eye. The eye on the opposite side of the head from a particular structure.

Convergence (neural). The process of many neurons synapsing onto fewer neurons.

Cornea. The transparent focusing element of the eye that is the first structure through which light passes as it enters the eye and that is the eye's major focusing element.

Dark adaptation. Visual adaptation that occurs in the dark, during which the sensitivity to light increases.

Dark adaptation curve. The function that traces the time course of the increase in visual sensitivity that occurs during dark adaptation.

Dark adapted sensitivity. The sensitivity of the eye after it has completely adapted to the dark.

Dorsal pathway. Pathway that conducts signals from the striate cortex to the parietal lobe. This has been called the "where" or the "how" pathway.

Duplicity theory of vision. The idea that the rod and cone receptors in the retina operate under different conditions and have different properties.

Electromagnetic energy. Energy radiated as waves that are produced by electric charges. The electromagnetic spectrum is a continuum of electromagnetic energy.

Electromagnetic spectrum. Continuum of electromagnetic energy that extends from very short wavelength gamma rays to long-wavelength radio waves. Visible light is a narrow band within this spectrum.

Enzyme cascade. Sequence of reactions triggered by an activated visual pigment molecule that results in transduction.

Excitatory-center-inhibitory-surround receptive field. A center-surround receptive field in which stimulation of the center area causes an excitatory response and stimulation of the surround causes an inhibitory response.

Extrastriate cortex. Areas in the cerebral cortex outside the striate cortex.

Extrastriate visual areas. Areas in the cortex that are activated by visual stimuli but are outside the striate cortex.

Focusing power. The degree to which a structure such as the lens or the cornea bends light. The greater the focusing power, the more the light passing through the structure is bent.

Fovea. A small area in the human retina that contains only cone receptors. The fovea is located on the line of sight, so that when a person looks at an object, its image falls on the fovea.

Ganglion cell. A neuron in the retina that receives inputs from bipolar and amacrine cells. The axons of the ganglion cells are the fibers that travel toward the lateral geniculate nucleus of the thalamus in the optic nerve.

Horizontal cell. A neuron that transmits signals laterally across the retina. Horizontal cells synapse with receptors and bipolar cells.

Inhibitory-center-excitatory-surround receptive field. A center-surround receptive field in which stimulation of the center causes an inhibitory response and stimulation of the surround causes an excitatory response.

Inhibitory response. The response of a nerve fiber in which the firing rate decreases due to inhibition from another neuron.

Ipsilateral eye. The eye on the same side of the head of the structure to which the eye sends inputs.

Isomerization. Change in shape of the retinal part of the visual pigment molecule that occurs when the molecule absorbs a quantum of light.

Lateral geniculate nucleus (LGN). The nucleus in the thalamus that receives inputs from the optic nerve and sends fibers to the cortical receiving area for vision.

Lateral inhibition. Inhibition that is spread laterally across a nerve circuit. In the retina, lateral inhibition is spread by the horizontal and amacrine cells.

Lateral plexus. A structure that transmits nerve impulses laterally in the Limulus eye.

Lens. The transparent focusing element of the eye through which light passes after passing through the cornea and the aqueous humor. The lens's change in shape to focus at different distances is called accommodation.

Light adapted sensitivity. The sensitivity of the light adapted eye.

Long-wavelength pigment. A cone visual pigment that absorbs light maximally at the long-wavelength end of the spectrum. In humans, this pigment absorbs maximally at 558 nm.

Mach bands. A perceptual effect that causes a thin dark band on the dark side of a light-dark border and a thin light band on the light side of the border even though corresponding intensity changes do not exist.

Medium-wavelength pigment. A cone visual pigment that absorbs light maximally in the middle of the spectrum. In humans, this pigment absorbs maximally at 531 nm.

Microspectrophotometry. A procedure for determining pigment absorption spectra that involves shining light through single receptors or through small numbers of receptors.

Monochromatic light. Light which contains only a single wavelength.

Near point. The distance at which the lens can no longer accommodate enough to bring close objects into focus. Objects nearer than the near point can be brought into focus only by corrective lenses.

Neural circuit. A number of neurons that are connected by synapses, usually involving a combination of excitatory and inhibitory connections.

Off-response. A burst of firing when a stimulus is turned off.

Ommatidium. A structure in the eye of the Limulus that contains a small lens, located directly over a visual receptor. The Limulus eye is made up of hundreds of these ommatidia.

On response. The response of a nerve fiber in which there is an increase in the firing rate when the stimulus is turned on; the same as an excitatory response.

Opsin. The protein part of the visual pigment molecule, to which the light-sensitive retinal molecule is attached.

Optic array. The way the light of the environment is structured by the presence of objects, surfaces, and textures.

Optic disk. The disk-shaped area at the back of the eye where the optic nerve leaves the eye.

Optic nerve. Bundle of nerve fibers that carry impulses from the retina to the lateral geniculate nucleus and other structures. Each optic nerve contains about 1 million ganglion cell fibers.

Parietal lobe. A lobe at the top of the cortex that is the site of the cortical receiving area for touch.

Peripheral retina. All of the retina except the fovea and a small area surrounding the fovea.

Pigment bleaching. The process that begins when a visual pigment molecule absorbs light. The molecule changes shape, and the color of the rod visual pigment changes from red to transparent. Sometime, early in this process, visual transduction takes place.

Pigment epithelium. A layer of cells that lines the inside of the eyeball under the retina.

Pigment regeneration. The reconstruction of the visual pigment molecule from its bleached state to its original unbleached state.

Presbyopia ("old eye"). The inability of the eye to accommodate due to the hardening of the lens and a weakening of the ciliary muscles. It occurs as people get older.

Pupil. The small opening at the front of the eye.

Purkinje shift. The shift from cone spectral sensitivity to rod spectral sensitivity that takes place during dark adaptation.

Receptive field. A neuron's receptive field is the area on the receptor surface (the retina, for vision; the skin, for touch) that, when stimulated, affects the firing of that neuron. There are some exceptions, however, such as receptive fields for auditory space perception in the owl. In this case, the receptive fields are locations in space rather than areas on the receptor surface.

Retina. A complex network of cells that covers the inside back of the eye. These cells include the receptors, which generate an electrical signal in response to light, as well as the horizontal, bipolar, amacrine, and ganglion cells.

Retinal. The light-sensitive part of the visual pigment molecule.

Rod monochromat. A person who has a retina in which the only functioning receptors are rods.

Rod spectral sensitivity curve. A graph showing the rod system's sensitivity to light as a function of the light's wavelength.

Rod-cone break. The point on the dark adaptation curve at which vision shifts from cone vision to rod vision.

Rods. Rod-shaped receptors in the retina that are primarily responsible for vision at low levels of illumination. The rod system is extremely sensitive in the dark but cannot resolve fine details.

Sensitivity. 1.0 divided by the threshold for detecting a stimulus. Thus, lower thresholds correspond to higher sensitivities.

Short-wavelength pigment. The cone visual pigment that absorbs maximally at short wavelengths. In the human, this pigment absorbs maximally at about 419 nm.

Simultaneous contrast. The effect that occurs when surrounding one color with another changes the appearance of the surrounded color.

Simultaneous lightness contrast. Effect that occurs when one area is surrounded by another area that is either lighter or darker. The surrounding area changes the lightness of the area that is surrounded.

Spatial summation. The summation, or accumulation, of the effect of stimulation covers large area.

Spectral sensitivity. The sensitivity of visual receptors to different parts of the visible spectrum. (See Spectral sensitivity curve).

Spectral sensitivity curve. The function relating a subject's sensitivity to light to the wavelength of the light.

Spectrophotometer. A device that measures the amount of light absorbed by a substance as a function of wavelength. For vision, spectrophotometers are used to measure the amount of light absorbed by visual pigments.

Striate cortex. The visual receiving area of the cortex, located in the occipital lobe.

Superior colliculus. A structure at the base of the brain that is important in controlling eye movements. A small proportion of the nerve fibers in the optic nerve synapse in the superior colliculus.

Thalamus. A nucleus in the brain where neurons from all of the senses, except smell, synapse on their way to their cortical receiving areas.

Threshold, relative. The amount of stimulus energy that can just be detected, expressed relative to another threshold. For example, "The amount of energy needed to detect a 500-nm light is twice as high as the amount of energy needed to detect a 540-nm light. "

Transduction. In the senses, the transformation of environmental energy into electrical energy. For example, the retinal receptors transduce light energy into electrical energy.

Two-color threshold method. A method used by Stiles in which the thresholds for different wavelengths are measured with a test flash that is superimposed on an adapting field.

Ventral pathway. Pathway that conducts signals from the striate cortex to the temporal lobe. This has also been called the "what" pathway. (2, 4)

Visible light. The range of wavelengths in the electromagnetic spectrum, from about 350 to 700 nm, that humans can see.

Visual acuity. The ability to resolve small details.

Visual cortex. See visual receiving area.

Visual pigment. A light-sensitive molecule contained in the rod and cone outer segments. The reaction of this molecule to light results in the generation of an electrical response in the receptors.

Visual receiving area (or visual cortex). The area in the occipital lobe, also called the striate cortex, that receives inputs from the lateral geniculate nucleus.

Visual transduction. Transformation of light energy into electrical energy that occurs in the rod and cone receptors in the retina.

Wavelength. For light energy, the distance between one peak of a light wave and the next peak.

TEST YOURSELF

Fill in the identities of the structures indicated in the cross-sections of the eye and retina below. (see Figures 2.3 and 2.4 in the text to check your answers)

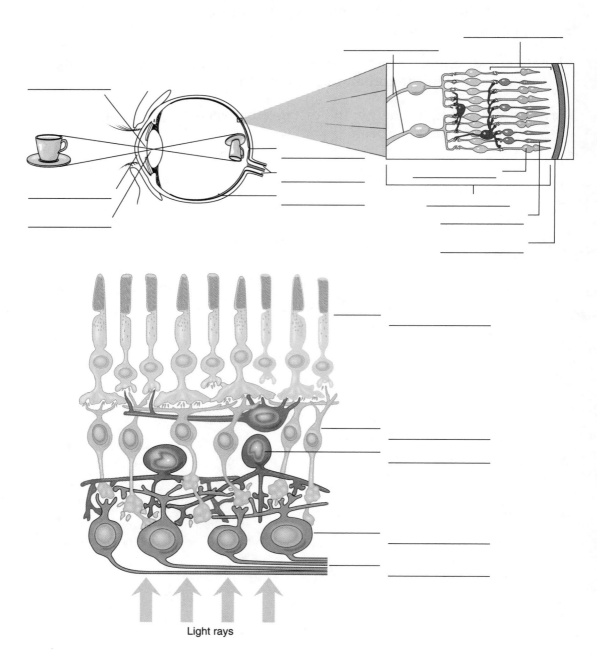

Light rays

42

The solid circle indicates the extent of the excitatory area of a center-surround receptive field. The dashed circle indicates the inhibitory surround. The shaded area indicates the area stimulated by light. Draw a picture of the neural response (use a vertical line to represent each action potential) on the lines below each receptive field. See Figure 2.36 to check your answer.

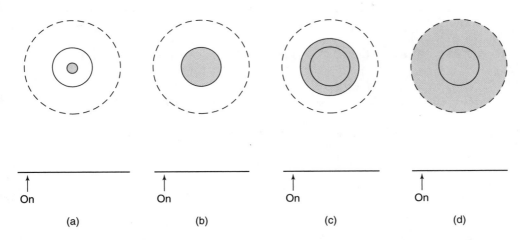

On   On   On   On

(a)   (b)   (c)   (d)

The circuit below indicates the initial output of each receptor in response to light. Each receptor sends inhibition to the receptor on either side. The inhibition equals one-fifth (0.2) of the initial output. Indicate the final output for each neuron at the end of the arrows. See Figure 2.47 for a similar calculation using a different amount of inhibition.

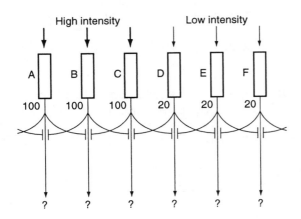

MULTIPLE-CHOICE QUESTIONS

2.1 A central theme of this book is that (1)
  a) perception is an illusion that we need to decode
  b) the key to understanding perception is measuring electrical signals in the nervous system
  c) perception is shaped by the operation of our perceptual systems
  d) perception can be measured in humans, but not in animals.

2.2 The visible spectrum is based on conceiving light as (3)
  a) traveling in waves
  b) made up of particles called photons

2.3 Light enters the eye by first passing through the (5)
  a) cornea
  b) lens
  c) pupil
  d) optic aperture

2.4 Moving a spot of light towards the eye (8)
  a) has no effect on the location of the focus point
  b) pushes the focus point back
  c) brings the focus point forward

2.5 Accommodation (9, 10)
  a) causes an increase in the focusing power of the eye
  b) decreases the curvature of the lens to bring near objects into focus
  c) is a psychological effect which blind people experience as they learn to deal with their visual problem
  d) decreases the focusing power of the lens

2.6 The receptors face "backwards" in the retina (13)
  a) to compensate for the fact that the image on the retina is inverted
  b) so they can make more efficient use of the incoming light
  c) so they can be in contact with the fovea
  d) so they can be in contact with the pigment epithelium

2.7 The visual pigments are located in (16)
     a) the receptor inner segments
     b) the opsin molecule
     c) the receptor outer segments
     d) the receptor wall

2.8 How many visual pigments molecules must be isomerized
     to excite a receptor? (18)
     a) 1
     b) 7
     c) 15
     d) 100

2.9 Immediately after the lights are turned off, the cones
     are _____ sensitive than the rods.(21)
     a) more
     b) less

2.10 Which situation below is not caused by lateral
     inhibition? (25)
     a) Mach bands
     b) simultaneous contrast
     c) increase of sensitivity during dark adaptation
     d) center-surround antagonism

2.11 The spectral sensitivity curves for rod and cone
     vision indicate that rod vision is more sensitive to
     _____ wavelength light than cone vision. (29)
     a) long
     b) short

2.12 The shape of the rod spectral sensitivity curve is
     determined by (30)
     a) the number of rod receptors in the retina
     b) the density of rod receptors in the retina
     c) the absorption spectrum of the rod visual pigment
     d) c and d

2.13 If we shine an intense light that contains long
     wavelengths into a person's eye and then measure the
     person's spectral sensitivity curve, we find that the
     resulting spectral sensitivity function has been
     shifted to ____ wavelengths compared to the normal
     cone spectral sensitivity curve. (33)
     a) shorter
     b) longer

2.14 The receptive field of a cell has an inhibitory center and excitatory surround. We will observe the highest firing rate from this cell when we (37)
a) stimulate only the center
b) stimulate only the surround
c) stimulate the entire receptive field
d) stimulate outside the receptive field

2.15 Which of the following is <u>not</u> a reason that rod vision is more sensitive than cone vision in the dark? (39)
a) the rods are packed more closely together
b) there is more neural convergence of signals from the rods
c) individual rod receptors generate larger responds than individual cone receptors

2.16 If convergence is high than spatial summation is (42)
a) low
b) high

2.17 Mach bands (49)
a) are decreases in the apparent brightness on the lighter side of a light-dark border
b) are increases in the apparent brightness on the darker side of a light-dark border
c) are caused by lateral inhibition
d) can be shown to occur in the Limulus (horseshoe crab) but are not observed by humans

2.18 The bands in the Mach band effect are (49)
a) physical
b) perceptual

2.19 Which of the following is <u>not</u> an example of how the properties of the <u>receptors</u> affect our perceptions? (49)
a) rapid initial phase of dark adaptation
b) acuity of cone vision
c) Mach card effect
d) greater sensitivity to short-wavelength light at dusk

CHAPTER 3

VISUAL PROCESSING:
THE LATERAL GENICULATE NUCLEUS
AND STRIATE CORTEX

In Chapter 2 we introduced the idea that perception is influenced by wiring - the way neurons are connected to one another. Chapter 3 continues this discussion of wiring but with an emphasis on the way this wiring is organized. The main message of this chapter is that the visual system is organized so neurons that respond to particular locations, orientations, and eyes, are located near each other in the visual system.

CHAPTER ORGANIZATION

1. How the lateral geniculate nucleus is organized in layers and the nature of the map of the retina on the LGN. This is called a retinotopic map.

2. How the striate cortex contains neurons that respond to specific types of stimuli.

3. How the cortex is organized into columns that contain neurons that process information about similar locations, orientations, and eye dominance.

4. How the environment is represented by nerve impulses - a representation which is called the sensory code.

TABLE OF CONTENTS AND KEY TERMS

Cortical Neurons As Spatial Frequency Analyzers
Psychophysical Evidence For Spatial Frequency Analyzers: Selective
Adaptation To Spatial Frequency
- **contrast sensitivity function**
- **spatial frequency channels**

The Striate Cortex: Organization Into Columns (88)
Location Columns And Retinal Maps
- **location column**
- **magnification factor**
Orientation Columns
- **orientation columns**
- **2-deoxyglucose technique**
Ocular Dominance Columns
- **ocular dominance**
- **ocular dominance columns**
Hypercolumns
- **hypercolumn**
- **processing module**

Sensory Coding: Making Sense Of The Neural Information (93)
- **specificity coding**
- **distributed coding**
- **mind-body problem**
Specificity Coding
Distributed Coding

Something To Consider: Representing Bill (96)

Across The Senses: Maps And Columns (98)
- **problem of sensory coding**
- **somatotopic map**
- **tonotopic map**
- **mind-body problem**

Study Questions (100)

NOTES: CHAPTER 3

<u>Organization of the LGN</u> (72)

The LGN is organized in layers and in columns. This organization is summarized in Table 3.1:

<u>Table 3.1</u>: Organization in the lateral geniculate nucleus

Basic Characteristic	How Organized In The LGN
Magnocellular fibers (From M-Ganglion cells)	In layers 1 and 2
Parvocellular fibers (From P-Ganglion cells)	In layers 3, 4, 5 & 6
Location on the retina	Retinotopic map on each layer of the LGN. This mapping is aligned so if an electrode oriented perpendicular to the surface of the LGN is lowered through the LGN, the receptive fields of the neurons along the track will all be on the same place on the retina.
Left or right eye	Ipsilateral eye (on same side as LGN) - Layers 2, 3, and 5 Contralateral eye (on opposite side from LGN) - Layers 1, 4, and 6.

Selective Neurons in the Cortex

One of the things we will encounter throughout the text is neurons that respond selectively to specific types of stimuli. The Table below lists the selective neurons described in this chapter.

Table 3.2: Selective neurons in the striate cortex

Stimulus Property	Type Of Cortical Neuron
Location (77)	Most cortical neurons have receptive fields at a particular location on the retina.
Orientation (77, 79)	Simple, complex, & end-stopped cells.
Direction of movement (77)	Complex & end stopped cells
Spatial frequency (82)	Spatial frequency-selective neurons

<u>Organization of the Visual Cortex</u> (88)

Like the LGN, the cortex also is organized in layers. However, in the cortex we are concerned not with the layered organization, but with <u>columnar organization</u>. The properties of the three types of columns in the cortex are summarized in Table 3.3.

<u>Table 3.3:</u> Columnar organization of the visual cortex

Basic Characteristic	How Organized In Cortex
Location (88)	• Similar to the LGN. There is a retinotopic map on the surface of the cortex, so each place on the cortex corresponds to a small area of retina. • Location columns exist so all neurons along the track of an electrode that is lowered into the cortex perpendicular to its surface have receptive fields that are on the same area of the retina.
Orientation (90)	All neurons in an orientation column have the same preferred orientation, so they respond best to stimuli with that orientation.
Ocular Dominance (91)	All neurons in an ocular dominance column have the same ocular dominance so they respond best to either the left or the right eye.

A key concept that it is important to understand with regard to these columns is how the columns are arranged in the cortex.

Location columns - Columns near each other have neurons with receptive fields near each other on the retina, as shown below:

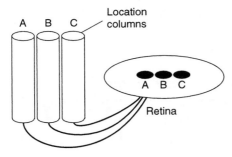

Orientation columns - Columns near each other have neurons with best orientations that are just slightly changed, as shown below:

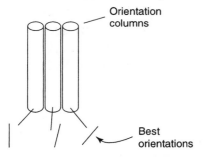

Ocular dominance columns - Columns for the left eye and the right eye are located next to each other for each place on the retina.

Combining the Columns: Within each location column, there is a set of orientation columns so that for each location there are neurons that respond to all orientations, as shown below:

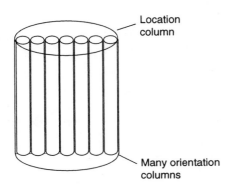

For each location on the retina, there is a <u>processing module</u> in the cortex which processes information from that location on the retina (see Figure 3.32). This processing module contains one location column, a set of all orientation columns, and left and right ocular dominance columns. This combination of columns, which processes information about stimuli that fall on a particular location on the retina, is called a <u>hypercolumn.</u>

<u>Sensory Coding</u> (93)

How does nerve firing represent various characteristics of the environment? That is the problem of sensory coding, and this problem is essentially what this book is about. For example, we want to know what pattern of nerve firing stands for "blue," what pattern stands for "round object," and so on.

This chapter introduces two approaches to the sensory code (1) specificity coding, which states that a particular characteristic is signaled by activity in a specific type of nerve fiber (so, for example, "blue" might be signaled by activity in fibers that fire only to blue), and (2) distributed coding, which states that a particular characteristic is signaled by the pattern of activity that is distributed across a number of nerve fibers.

While there are many neurons that are specialized to respond best to a specific type of stimulus, the sensory code for most sensory qualities is probably more accurately described as distributed coding, because a large number of nerve fibers usually fire in response to a particular stimulus. There are other reasons, as well, for believing that distributed coding is the dominant form of coding for the senses (see pages 94-96).

Mind-Body Problem (94)

Students often confuse the problem of sensory coding and the mind-body problem. Most research on sensory coding is concerned with determining the relationship between the <u>stimulus</u> and the <u>physiological response</u>. So a researcher studying sensory coding might look at the relationship between a vertical bar of light and the response that this bar causes in the cortex.

The mind-body problem is concerned with the relationship between the <u>physiological response</u> and the <u>essence of our experience</u>. So a researcher studying the mind-body problem might ask how a particular pattern of nerve firing causes the experience of "blueness." In other words, how does the jump occur between physical processes (like nerve impulses) and perceptual responses (like experiencing "blue.")? Another way to look at the mind-body problem is to remember that nerve impulses are actually sodium and potassium ions flowing across the nerve membrane (see Chapter 1 in the text). The mind-body problem asks how this flow of charged molecules could give rise to a sensory experience. The difficulty involved in solving the mind-body problem, has caused most researchers to focus not on the mind-body problem, but on sensory coding.

KEY TERMS: CHAPTER 3

2-Deoxyglucose technique. An anatomical technique that makes it possible to see which neurons in a structure have been activated. For example, this technique was used to visualize the orientation columns in the visual cortex.

Columnar arrangement. The arrangement of neurons with similar properties in columns perpendicular to the surface of the cortex. For example, there are location, orientation, and ocular dominance columns in the visual system and frequency columns in the auditory system.

Complex cell. A neuron in the visual cortex that responds best to moving bars with a particular orientation.

Contralateral eye. The eye on the opposite side of the head from a particular structure.

Contrast. The difference in light intensity between two areas. For a visual grating stimulus, the contrast is the amplitude of the grating divided by its mean intensity.

Contrast sensitivity. Sensitivity to the difference in the light intensities in two adjacent areas. Contrast sensitivity is usually measured by taking the reciprocal of the minimum intensity difference between two bars of a grating necessary to see the bars.

Contrast sensitivity function (CSF). A plot of contrast sensitivity versus the spatial frequency of a grating stimulus.

Distributed coding. Type of neural code in which different perceptions are signaled by the pattern of activity that is distributed across many neurons (see specificity coding).

End-stopped cell. A cortical neuron that responds best to lines of a specific length that are moving in a particular direction.

Feature detector. A neuron that responds selectively to a specific feature of the stimulus.

Fourier analysis. A mathematical technique that analyzes complex periodic waveforms into a number of sine-wave components.

Grating. A stimulus pattern consisting of alternating bars with different lightnesses or colors.

Hypercolumn. A column of cortex about 1 mm on a side that contains a location column for a particular area of the retina, left and right ocular dominance columns, and a complete set of orientation columns. A hypercolumn can be thought of as a processing module for a particular location on the retina.

Ipsilateral eye. The eye on the same side of the head of the structure to which the eye sends inputs.

Location column. A column in the visual cortex that contains neurons with the same receptive field locations on the retina.

M-cells. Retinal ganglion cells that have medium sized cell bodies and which respond with sustained firing. M-cells synapse in the magnocellular layer of the LGN.

Magnification factor. The apportioning of proportionally more space on the cortex to the representation of specific areas of sensory receptors. For example, a small area on the retina in or near the fovea receives more space on the cortex than the same area of peripheral retina. Similarly, the fingertips receive more space on the somatosensory cortex than the forearm or leg.

Magnocellular (or magno). Neurons in layers 1 and 2 of the lateral geniculate nucleus that receive inputs from the M ganglion cells.

Mind-body problem. The problem of how physical processes such as nerve impulses cause mental processes such as perceptual experience.

Ocular dominance. The degree to which a neuron is influenced by stimulation of each eye. A neuron has a large amount of ocular dominance if it responds only to stimulation of one eye. There is no ocular dominance if the neuron responds equally to stimulation of both eyes.

Ocular dominance column. A column in the visual cortex that contains neurons with the same ocular dominance.

Orientation. The angle of a stimulus relative to vertical.

Orientation column. A column in the visual cortex that contains neurons with the same orientation preference.

Orientation tuning curve. A function relating the firing rate of a neuron to the orientation of the stimulus.

P-cells. Retinal ganglion cells that have larger cell bodies than the M-cells and which respond with brief bursts of firing. P-cells synapse in the parvocellular area of the LGN.

Parvocellular (or parvo). Neurons in layers 3, 4, 5, and 6 of the lateral geniculate nucleus. These neurons receive inputs from the P ganglion cells.

Problem of sensory coding. The problem of determining what characteristics of neural firing represent specific stimuli in the environment. For example, researchers have asked what pattern of nerve firing stands for "blue" or "red."

Processing module. A term used in Chapter 3 to refer to hypercolumns, each of which processes information from a small area of the retina.

Retinotopic map. A map on a structure in the visual system, such as the lateral geniculate nucleus or the cortex, that indicates locations on the structure that correspond to locations on the retina. In retinotopic maps, locations adjacent to each other on the retina are usually represented by locations that are adjacent to each other on the structure.

Selective adaptation. A procedure in which a person or animal is selectively exposed to one stimulus and then the effect of this exposure is assessed by testing with a wide range of stimuli. Exposing a person to vertical bars and then testing a person's sensitivity to bars of all orientations is an example of selective adaptation to orientation. Selective adaptation can also be carried out for spatial frequency, wavelength, and speech sounds.

Sensory coding, problem of See Problem of sensory coding.

Simple cortical cell. A neuron in the visual cortex that responds best to bars of a particular orientation.

Sine-wave grating. A grating stimulus with a sine-wave intensity distribution.

Somatotopic map. A map created on the somatosensory area of the brain by the arrangement of neurons so that neurons that respond to adjacent parts of the body are found next to each other on the brain.

Spatial frequency. For a grating stimulus, spatial frequency refers to the frequency with which the grating repeats itself per degree of visual angle. For more natural stimuli, high spatial frequencies are associated with fine details, and low spatial frequencies are associated with grosser features.

Spatial frequency channels. Hypothesized channels in the visual system that are sensitive to narrow ranges of spatial frequencies.

Specificity coding. Type of neural code in which different perceptions are signaled by activity in specific neurons (see Distributed coding).

Square-wave grating. A grating stimulus with a square-wave intensity distribution.

Tuning curve, orientation. See Orientation tuning curve.

Waveform. A waveform describes functions in which stimulus intensity or amplitude is plotted versus time or space. For example, we can describe the waveform of a pure tone stimulus (a plot of pressure change vs. time) as a sine wave, or we can refer to the waveform of a grating stimulus (a plot of light intensity vs. distance) as a sine wave or a square wave.

TEST YOURSELF

MULTIPLE CHOICE QUESTIONS

3.1 Ellen looks at Bill and seem him. We say that she perceives Bill indirectly because (3)
   a) her perception is based on the firing of nerve impulses
   b) she can only see part of him at a time
   c) he is located at a distance from her
   d) according to some philosophers, life might, in fact, be a very convincing illusion

3.2 Receptive fields of LGN neurons are arranged in a _____ configuration. (4)
   a) center-surround
   b) side-by-side
   c) homogeneous (the same all over)

3.3 We are recording from a neuron in the lateral geniculate nucleus that is located on the left side of the brain. In this situation, which is the ipsilateral eye? (7)
   a) the left eye
   b) the right eye

3.4 Which structure has been called a "club sandwich?" (10)
   a) retina
   b) lateral geniculate nucleus
   c) visual cortex
   d) BLT nucleus

3.5 Each layer of the LGN receives inputs from (11)
   a) M & P ganglion cells
   b) only one of the eyes
   c) either the M or the P ganglion cells, but not both
   d) both b and c

3.6 Simple cells have receptive fields that (16)
   a) have side-by-side excitatory and inhibitory areas
   b) are center-surround
   c) respond only to a moving stimulus
   d) are located in the lateral geniculate nucleus

3.7 To obtain the maximum response from a(n) _____ cell
     the retina must be stimulated with a moving line with
     a specific length. (17)
     a) center-surround
     b) simple
     c) complex
     d) end-stopped

3.8 Contrast sensitivity measures an observer's ability to
     see (21)
     a) a flashing test light in the dark
     b) small details on an eye chart
     c) the smallest difference in intensity that can be
        detected between light and dark bars in a grating
     d) when both the center and surround of their
        receptive field has been stimulated simultaneously

3.9 The results of selective adaptation experiments with
     gratings of different orientations suggest that (19,
     23)
     a) there are orientation columns in the visual cortex
     b) it may not be valid to generalize from the results
        of physiological experiments on animals to humans
     c) feature detectors play only a minor role in human
        perception
     d) feature detectors may play a role in human
        perception

3.10 According to the "thumb method" of measuring visual
     angle (25)
     a) the thumb at arms length covers about 2 degrees on
        the retina
     b) the image of the thumb at arms length takes up
        about 1 degree of visual angle
     c) when the thumb is placed in contact with an object,
        it covers about 2 degrees of visual angle
     d) none of the above

3.11 If you are viewing the roof of a house from above, the
     array of small shingles would have a _____ spatial
     frequency (29)
     a) low
     b) high

3.12 The contrast sensitivity function is a plot of (31)
   a) contrast versus spatial frequency
   b) bar width versus threshold
   c) contrast sensitivity versus wavelength
   d) contrast sensitivity versus spatial frequency

3.13 If we record from neurons along an electrode track
   that penetrates obliquely to the surface of the visual
   cortex (38)
   a) we will be in a location column
   b) we will encounter neurons with superimposed
      receptive fields
   c) the receptive fields of the neurons we encounter
      will be systematically displaced from each other
   d) a and b

3.14 Two neurons in the same location column (39)
   a) are located side-by-side on the cortex
   b) will have receptive fields that are side by side on
      the retina
   c) will have receptive fields on the same place on the
      retina
   d) will all be the same kind of neuron (simple,
      complex, end stopped.)

3.15 Ten ganglion cells leaving the fovea will send their
   signals to a larger area on the cortex than ten
   ganglion cells in the periphery (41)
   a) True
   b) False

3.16 The density of neurons in the visual cortex (42)
   a) is the same in all areas of the visual cortex
   b) is higher in areas receiving fibers from the
      peripheral retina
   c) is higher in areas receiving fibers from the fovea

3.17 A long bar-shaped stimulus presented to the retina
   causes a long bar-shaped pattern of excitation in the
   striate cortex. (49)
   a) True
   b) False

CHAPTER 4

HIGHER-LEVEL VISUAL PROCESSING

Chapter 4 is the last of the chapters that introduce basic physiological principles. In this chapter we consider new research which has shown that substantial processing of visual information occurs in an area called the extrastriate cortex, which consists of a number of structures outside of the striate cortex that respond to visual stimuli.

CHAPTER ORGANIZATION

1. How the extrastriate cortex is organized

    (a) into two "streams" - the dorsal stream from the striate cortex to the parietal lobe (top of the brain), and the ventral stream from the striate cortex to the temporal lobe (side of the brain).

    (b) into modules - structures that are specialized to process information about specific perceptual qualities such as motion, form, and color. These structures contain individual neurons that respond selectively to specific stimulus properties.

2. How neuropsychological research, which looks at how brain damage affects human perception, reaches similar conclusions about processing streams and modularity as the research above, which is based largely on animal research.

3, How neural responding is influenced by attention.

4. How the information in the neural response that a particular object causes in many areas throughout the cortex, is combined to create a perception of a whole coherent object (The binding problem).

TABLE OF CONTENTS AND KEY TERMS

Modular Organization (109)

The <u>main message</u> of Chapter 4 is that at higher levels, cortical organization is <u>modular</u>. That is, specific structures are specialized to process information about specific perceptual qualities. The text describes modular organization in three structures, all of which are in either the dorsal or ventral extrastriate pathways (see Figure 4.4, page 106).

<u>Table 4.1</u> Modular structures in the extrastriate cortex

Structure	Extrastriate Stream	Quality
Medial Temporal (MT)	Dorsal	Movement
Inferotemporal (IT)	Ventral	Form
V4	Ventral	Color

Selective Neurons (Continued from Chapter 3) (110-113)

In Chapter 3 we saw that there were neurons in the striate cortex that respond best to specific stimuli. Table 4.2 indicates neurons in the inferotemporal (IT) cortex that also respond to specific stimuli.

Table 4.2: Selective neurons in the IT cortex.

Stimulus Property	Type Of Cortical Neuron
Simple shape	Primary cell
Complex shape	Elaborate cell
Different sizes of the same shape	Size-invariant cell
Different locations of the same shape	Location-invariant cell (have very large receptive fields)
Different views of a face	View-invariant face cell
A particular view of a face	View-specific face cell

Bimodal and Body-Centered Neurons (124)

Not all neurons respond to just one sense. The Across the Senses section at the end of this chapter describes bimodal neurons that respond both to visual and tactile stimuli. Neurons such as this, that respond to more than one sense, probably help us coordinate our actions across different senses. For our purposes, the most significant thing about the neurons described on pages 124-125 is that they expand our definition of the receptive field.

Remember that we defined a cell's receptive field as the <u>area on the retina that influences the firing of the cell</u>. Let's consider how this might work for a bimodal neuron in the monkey's cortex that responds both to touching the hand and to a visual stimulus. Any time we touch the hand we get a response. In addition, we also get a response to a visual stimulus that is presented in an area of space near the hand. But since the hand can move, this means that this cell responds when we stimulate many different places on the retina, as shown below:

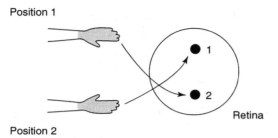

This type of cell does not exactly fit our original definition of the receptive field, since the key defining feature of what makes the neuron fire is not the area on the retina that is stimulated, but the part of the body that is stimulated. That is why this type of cell is called a *body-centered* neuron. Note that the receptive field is <u>still</u> always associated with the place where the stimulus is. That is, the receptive field is not located <u>at</u> the neuron from which we are recording, but it is a property <u>of</u> the neuron.

KEY TERMS: CHAPTER 4

Attention. The process of seeking out stimuli that are of interest

Bimodal neurons. Neurons that responds to stimulation of two senses. For example, a neuron that responds to both visual and tactual stimulation.

Binding problem. The problem of how neural activity in many separated areas in the brain is combined to create a perception of a coherent object.

Binocular rivalry. The situation that occurs when two different images are presented to the left and right eyes and perception alternates back and forth between the two images.

Blindsight. A situation in which a person can't see a light at a particular place in the visual field but can indicate that a stimulus is at that location by pointing or by other means.

Body-centered neurons. Neurons that have visual receptive fields that respond when a visual stimulus is presented near a particular part of the body.

Cell assembly. A group of neurons that fire together in response to a particular stimulus.

Covert awareness. An awareness of a stimulus that appears to happen "under the surface" of conscious perception. Blindsight is an example of covert awareness.

Dissociation, double. In brain damage, when function A is present and function B is absent, and, in another person, when function A is absent and function B is present. Presence of a double dissociation means that the two functions involve different mechanisms and operate independently of one another.

Dissociation, single. When, as a result of brain damage, one function is present and another is absent. Existence of a single dissociation indicates that the two functions involve different mechanisms, but may not be totally independent of one another.

Dorsal pathway. Pathway that conducts signals from the striate cortex to the parietal lobe. This has been called the "where" or the "how" pathway.

Double dissociation. See Dissociation, double.

Elaborate cells. Neurons in the IT cortex that respond best to complex stimuli such as specific shapes or shapes combined with a color or texture. (See Primary cells).

Extrastriate cortex. Areas in the cerebral cortex outside the striate cortex.

Extrastriate visual areas. Areas in the cortex that are activated by visual stimuli but are outside the striate cortex.

Location-invariant neurons. Neurons that respond to a stimulus over large areas of the retina.

Modularity. Specialization of the brain in which specific cortical areas processes information about specific perceptual qualities.

Module. A structure that processes information about a specific behavior or perceptual quality. Often identified as a structure that contains a large proportion of neurons that respond selectively to a particular quality .

Multimodal neurons. Neurons that respond to stimulation by more than one sense modality.

Multimodal neurons. Neurons that responds to stimulation of two or more senses.

Neuropsychology. The study of how brain damage affects a person's behavior.

Perimetry. A technique in which a small spot of light is presented to different areas of the visual field, to determine areas in which subjects can and cannot perceive the spot. Used to determine the location and extent of scotomas.

Positron emission tomography. A technique that can be used in aware human subjects to determine which brain areas are activated by various tasks.

Primary cells. Neurons in the IT cortex that respond best to simple stimuli like slits, spots, ellipses, and squares. (See Elaborate cells).

Prosopagnosia. A form of visual agnosia in which the person can't recognize faces.

Scotoma. An area of blindness in the visual field, usually caused by retinal or cortical damage.

Single dissociation. See Dissociation, single.

Size-invariant neurons. Neurons that respond equally well to stimuli of various sizes.

Ventral pathway. Pathway that conducts signals from the striate cortex to the temporal lobe. This has also been called the "what" pathway. (2, 4)

View-invariant cells. Neurons that respond equally well to different views of an object. View-invariant cells for faces have been found in IT cortex. (See View-specific cells).

View-specific cells. Neurons that respond best to specific views of a stimulus. View-specific cells that respond best to specific views of faces have been found in IT cortex. (See View-invariant cells).

TEST YOURSELF

In the figure below add the names of the structures indicated by the empty boxes. See Figure 4.4 to check your answer.

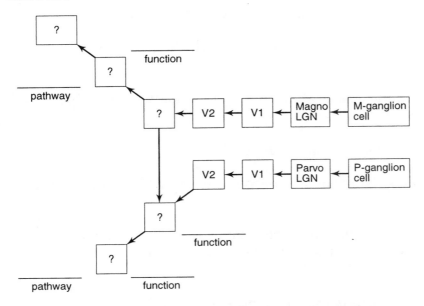

MULTIPLE-CHOICE QUESTIONS

4.1 The striate cortex is the main "perceptive center" for human visual perception. (1)
a) True
b) False

4.2 "Dorsal" refers to _____ in humans. (3)
a) the back of the body and top of the head
b) the front of the body and front of the head

4.3 A monkey with its parietal lobes removed will have difficulty solving _____ problem. (4, 5)
a) an object discrimination
b) a landmark discrimination

4.4 If a single dissociation occurs between two functions, this means that the two functions (10)
a) involve different mechanisms
b) operate independently of each other
c) have the same mechanism
d) a and b

4.5 Goodale's patient D.F., who had ventral lobe damage and who identified a screwdriver as "a long black thin" had (11)
a) prosopagnosia
b) object recognition deficit
c) visual form agnosia
d) visuo-motor agnosia

4.6 Which area below contains the largest population of directionally selective neurons? (14)
a) Striate cortex
b) MT
c) V4
d) IT

4.7 Lesioning a monkey's medial temporal (MT) cortex (14, 18)
a) decreases the monkey's ability to see forms
b) increases the monkey's threshold for detecting the direction of movement
c) decreases the monkeys ability to see color
d) makes it easier for the monkey to detect small changes in the direction of movement

4.8 The inferotemporal cortex is concerned largely with perceiving (16)
a) form
b) movement
c) color
d) depth

4.9 Research has shown that our perception of a particular face may be based on the firing of one highly specific face cell.(21)
a) True
b) False

4.10 In Rock and Guttman's experiment, in which they showed
subjects two superimposed forms and had them pay
attention to one of them, the conclusion was that (32)
a) it is possible to attend to two things at once.
b) we are unaware of things that we ignore
c) physiological responses are stronger to the
attended form
d) paying attention directs our receptors to what we
want to perceive

4.11 The binding problem is concerned with (34)
a) how the nervous system combines the information in
different cortical locations
b) the relationship between psychophysical and
physiological responding
c) how attention "binds" an objects characteristics to
a specific place in memory
d) combining stimuli and cognitive processes to result
in perception

4.12 In a binocular rivalry experiment, the stimulus _____
change its position on the retina.(38)
a) does
b) does not

CHAPTER 5

PERCEIVING COLOR

Congratulations. You have finished the "Introductory" section of the book. If you have mastered all of the concepts in Chapters 1 - 4, you know most of the physiological principles necessary to understand the material in the rest of the book. We will also be adding a few perceptual principles, in this chapter and those that follow.

The main purposes of this chapter are: (1) to describe basic research on the sensory code for color, and (2) to show how early perceptual researchers were able to determine physiological mechanisms for color vision based on behavioral evidence.

CHAPTER ORGANIZATION

1. How we describe color and the relationship between our perception of color and the wavelengths of light.

2. How behavioral evidence was used in the 1800's to create two physiological theories of color vision - trichromatic theory and opponent-process theory.

3. How physiological research has confirmed and redefined the physiological mechanisms proposed by the early researchers.

4. What happens when there is an abnormality in the physiological mechanism for color vision.

TABLE OF CONTENTS AND KEY TERMS

NOTES: CHAPTER 5

Deducing Physiological Mechanisms from Behavioral Results

Color perception provides an excellent example of how it is possible to deduce physiological mechanisms from behavioral findings, as summarized in Table 5.1:

Table 5.1: Deducing physiological mechanisms from behavioral evidence

Behavioral Evidence	Physiological Conclusion	Physiological Evidence
Color Matching - People with normal color vision can match any wavelength by mixing three others	There are three types of receptors responsible for color vision (trichromatic theory)	Microspectrophoto-metry. There are three different cone pigments, each of which absorbs light best in a specific region of the spectrum.

Table continued on next page . . . .

Table 5.1 (Continued)

Behavioral Evidence	Physiological Conclusion	Physiological Evidence
• Afterimages - Red causes a green afterimage; Blue causes a yellow afterimage. • Color deficiency. People tend to lose the ability to perceive red and green together; blue and yellow together. • Simultaneous contrast. Surrounding a gray field with red, causes a perception of green. Blue and yellow are also paired. • It is hard to imagine blue and yellow in the same color, or red and green in the same color.	There are "opponent processes" that respond in opposite ways to blue and yellow, red and green (opponent-process theory)	• Opponent neurons in the LGN. • Type 1 color opponent cells and double color opponent cells in the cortex.

Neural Circuits for Color Perception (146)

Color vision also provides an example of how responding can be determined by neural circuits. Figure 5.19 on page 146 shows a simple neural circuit that creates opponent neurons from inputs from the short-, medium-, and long-wavelength cones. Consider the two hypothetical circuits below (remember that the Y's are excitatory synapses and the T's are inhibitory synapses) and try to figure out how each of the neurons A, B, and C would respond to stimulation with short-, medium-, and long-wavelength light.

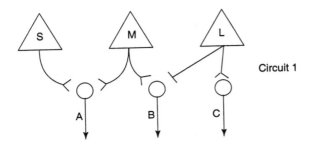

Circuit 1

In Circuit 1, neuron A would be excited by a broad band of wavelengths from the short- and middle-wavelength regions of the spectrum since both the short and medium wavelength cones make excitatory synapses with this neuron. Note that this is not an opponent neuron. Neuron B is like a G+R- neuron. It is excited by medium- wavelength light and inhibited by long wavelengths. Neuron C is excited by long wavelengths. It, too, is not an opponent neuron.

80

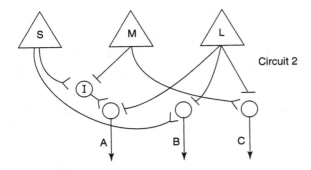

Circuit 2

In Circuit 2, neuron A is excited by short wavelengths, since stimulation of the short-wavelength cone excites neuron I which then excites A. But if medium wavelength is presented simultaneously with short-wavelength light the neuron decreases firing since the medium-wavelength cone inhibits cell I. Note that presenting medium wavelength light alone has little effect on neuron A. If the medium-wavelength cone had synapsed directly on A, medium wavelength light would cause a decrease in neuron A's spontaneous activity. Neuron A is also inhibited by long wavelength light, since it receives an inhibitory input from the long-wavelength cone. Neuron B is excited by short-wavelengths and inhibited by long wavelengths; Neuron C is excited by medium wavelengths and inhibited by long wavelengths.

Physiological Influence and Creating Experience (150)
Color also invites us to look at two ways that physiology affects what we perceive. We know from both the evidence for trichromatic and opponent-process theories that the visual pigments and neural wiring influence what we perceive in a number of ways. For example, the existence of three cone pigments causes us to be able to match any wavelength by mixing a minimum of three other wavelengths.

But the discussion in the Something to Consider section on page 150 goes beyond influencing to creating. According to the discussion in this section, a 420 nm light is not really blue. It is just electromagnetic energy with a wavelength of 420 nm. If you hadn't been told that 420 nm light usually looks blue, you wouldn't have any way of knowing it was blue (without looking to see what color it was).

The "blueness" is put into the 420-nm light by the operation of the nervous system. Something about the pattern of nerve firing causes us to experience blues, red, orange and all of the other colors. But the colors are not contained in the light energy - they are <u>created</u> by the nervous system. So when you consider how physiology affects perception, remember that it can affect it in at least two different ways: (1) It can <u>influence</u> what we perceive (Example: We can match any wavelength by mixing three other wavelengths); and (2) It can <u>create</u> the essence of what we experience (Example: a 420-nm light looks blue, a 630-nm light looks red).

KEY TERMS: CHAPTER 5

Achromatic color. Colors without hue; white, black, and all the grays between these two extremes are achromatic colors.

Additive color mixture. See Color mixture, additive.

Afterimage. An image that is perceived after the original source of stimulation is removed. A visual afterimage usually occurs after one views a high-contrast stimulus for 30 to 60 seconds.

Anomalous trichromat. A person who needs to mix a minimum of three wavelengths to match any other wavelength in the spectrum but mixes these wavelengths in different proportions from a trichromat.

Blobs. Cells found in areas of the visual cortex that take up a stain that selectively colors areas that contain the enzyme cytochromeoxidase. Many of these cells have double color-opponent receptive fields.

Chromatic adaptation. The adaptation of the eye to chromatic light. Chromatic adaptation is selective adaptation to wavelengths in a particular region of the visible spectrum.

Chromatic color. Colors with hue, such as blue, yellow, red, and green.

Color deficiency. People with color deficiency (sometimes incorrectly called color blindness) see fewer colors than people with normal color vision and need to mix fewer wavelengths to match any other wavelength in the spectrum.

Color mixing. Combining two or more different colors to create a new color. See Color mixture, additive, and Color mixture, subtractive.

Color mixture, additive. The result when lights of different colors are superimposed.

Color mixture, subtractive. The result when paints of different colors are mixed together.

Color, achromatic. See achromatic color.

Color, chromatic. See chromatic color.

Color-matching experiment. A procedure in which observers are asked to match the color in one field by mixing two or more lights in another field.

Color-opponent cells, type 1. Cortical cell which has a center-surround receptive field that is inhibited by one band of wavelengths presented to the surround, and excited by another band presented to the center (or visa versa).

Color-opponent cells, double. A cell with a center-surround receptive field that responds in an opponent manner to stimulation of the field's center with reversed opponent response to stimulation of the surround. For example if the center response is R+G- the surround response will be R-G+.

Color. A perceptual response to objects and lights that causes them to possess qualities such as redness, greenness, whiteness, and grayness.

Deuteranopia. A form of red-green color dichromatism caused by lack of the middle-wavelength cone pigment.

Dichromat. A person who has a form of color deficiency. Dichromats can match any wavelength in the spectrum by mixing two other wavelengths. Deuteranopes, protanopes, and tritanopes are all dichromats.

Double color-opponent cell. See Color-opponent cells, double.

Hue. The experience of a chromatic color such as red, green, yellow, or blue or combinations of these colors.

Ishihara plate. A display made up of colored dots used to test for the presence of color deficiency. The dots are colored so that people with normal (trichromatic) color vision can perceive numbers in the plate, but people with color deficiency cannot perceive these numbers or perceive different numbers from someone with trichromatic vision.

Medium-wavelength pigment. A cone visual pigment that absorbs light maximally in the middle of the spectrum. In humans, this pigment absorbs maximally at 531 nm.

Metamers. Two lights that have different wavelength distributions but are perceptually identical.

Neutral point. The wavelength at which a dichromat perceives gray.

Monochromat. A person who is completely color-blind and therefore sees everything as black, white, or shades of gray. A monochromat can match any wavelength in the spectrum by adjusting the intensity of any other wavelength.

Opponent cell. A neuron that has an excitatory response to wavelengths in one part of the spectrum and an inhibitory response to wavelengths in the other part of the spectrum. (See Color-opponent cell)

Opponent-process theory of color vision. A theory stating that our perception of color is determined by the activity of two opponent mechanisms: a blue-yellow mechanism and a red-green mechanism. The responses to the two colors in each mechanism oppose each other, one being an excitatory response and the other an inhibitory response. (This theory also includes a black-white mechanism, which is concerned with the perception of brightness.)

Perceptual segregation. Perceptual organization in which one object is seen as separate from other objects.

Protanopia. A form of red-green dichromatism caused by a lack of the long-wavelength cone pigment.

Reflectance. The percentage of light reflected from a surface.

Reflectance curve. A plot showing the percentage of light reflected from an object versus wavelength.

Saturation (color). The relative amount of whiteness in a chromatic color. The less whiteness a color contains, the more saturated it is.

Selective reflection. When an object reflects some wavelengths of the spectrum more than others.

S-potential. A slow electrical response recorded from neurons in the fish retina that has opponent properties. (See Opponent cell)

Subtractive color mixture. See Color mixture, subtractive.

Trichromat. A person with normal color vision. Trichromats can match any wavelength in the spectrum by mixing three other wavelengths in various proportions.

Trichromatic theory of color vision. A theory postulating that our perception of color is determined by the ratio of activity in three cone receptor mechanisms with different spectral sensitivities.

Tritanopia. A form of dichromatism thought to be caused by a lack of the short-wavelength cone pigment.

Tungsten light. Light produced by a tungsten filament. Tungsten light has a wavelength distribution that has relatively more intensity at long wavelengths than at short wavelengths.

Unilateral dichromat. A person who has dichromatic vision in one eye and trichromatic vision in the other eye.

Wavelength distribution. The amount of energy in a light at each of the wavelengths in the spectrum.

White light. Light that contains an equal intensity of each of the visible wavelengths.

Young-Helmholtz theory of color vision. See Trichromatic theory of color vision.

TEST YOURSELF

The three curves below indicate how the short, medium, and long-wavelength cones respond across the visible spectrum. From these curves, indicate how these three cones would respond to 450-, 500-, and 550-nm lights.

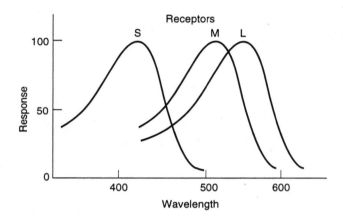

| Wavelength | Cone Pigment Response | | |
	Short	Medium	Long
450			
500			
550			

MULTIPLE CHOICE QUESTIONS

5.1 Which of the following is the most important function of color vision, according to the text? (1)
a) aesthetic functions
b) signaling
c) perceptual organization
d) detection of predators

5.2 Adding white to a color (5)
a) decreases its intensity
b) decreases its brightness
c) increases its saturation
d) decreases its saturation

5.3 Cross-cultural studies show that _____ is the first chromatic color term to appear in all languages. (7)
a) red
b) blue
c) orange
d) brown

5.4 Objects that reflect predominately long and medium wavelength light usually appear (12)
a) yellow
b) blue
c) red
d) green

5.5 The results of color matching experiments show that a person with normal color vision can match any wavelength in the spectrum by mixing ____ other wavelengths in the correct proportions (pick the smallest number that is correct) (13)
a) 2
b) 3
c) 4
d) 5

5.6 Which theory of color vision was initially proposed based primarily on phenomenological observations? (15, 16)
a) specificity
b) opponent-process
c) trichromatic

5.7 Which of the following is <u>least</u> associated with the opponent-process theory of color vision? (15, 16)
a) afterimages
b) LGN cells that are inhibited by red and excited by green
c) simultaneous contrast
d) three types of cones

5.8 Two objects that reflect different distributions of wavelengths will always appear different in color.(21)
a) True
b) False

5.9 A difference in one amino acid in the visual pigment's opsin molecule, causes a shift of about ____ nm in the peak of a pigment's absorption spectrum.   (24)
a) 2
b) 6
c) 10
d) 20

5.10 Research has shown that some subjects with normal trichromatic vision have four different cone pigments.(25)
a) True
b) False

5.11 Each cortical column associated with color contains neurons that (31)
a) are all sensitive to one basic color (blue, red, green, et.)
b) respond to similar orientations and have similar opponent properties
c) respond best to color mixtures
d) are all the same type of opponent cell (B-Y or R-G)

5.12 Which of the following needs only two wavelengths to match any other color? (37, 38)
a) monochromat
b) anomalous trichromat
c) protanope
d) b and c

5.13 Color deficiency is (40)
    a) equally distributed between males and females
    b) more prevalent in males
    c) more prevalent in females

5.14 The "neutral point" is the point at which a dichromat (41)
    a) perceives all colors of the spectrum
    b) perceives the color to which he is supposedly blind
    c) perceives gray or white
    d) can match any color by mixing together any two other colors

5.15 Light rays of specific wavelengths are simply energy and actually have no color at all.(43)
    a) True
    b) False

5.16 From our knowledge of the bee's visual pigments we can predict that bees will perceive blue in the ultraviolet (very short wavelength) part of the spectrum. (45)
    a) True
    b) False

5.17 Adding a color to a substance always hampers taste identification (49, 50)
    a) True
    b) False

CHAPTER 6

PERCEPTUAL CONSTANCY

This chapter is about a number of different "constancies." But the basic message behind all of them are the same: Under most normal conditions our perception tends to conform to the object's properties and not to the nature of the energy received by our retinal receptors.

CHAPTER ORGANIZATION

This chapter considers each type of constancy - color, lightness, shape, and size - first describing the phenomenon and then the mechanisms that keep our perception stable under changing environmental conditions. Size constancy is introduced in this chapter, and is described in more detail in Chapter 9.

TABLE OF CONTENTS AND KEY TERMS

NOTES: CHAPTER 6

The types of perceptual constancy discussed in this chapter are summarized in Table 6.1

Table 6.1: Types of perceptual constancy

Quality Perceived	Perception Usually Corresponds To	Stimulus on Retina Can Be Changed By . . .	Mechanisms That Keep Perception Constant
Color (Red, green, blue, etc.)	Wavelengths reflected from object	Illuminating object with different wavelengths	• Chromatic adaptation • Surroundings are also illuminated • Memory color
Lightness (Black, gray, white)	Albedo (percentage of light reflected from object)	Illuminating object with more or less light.	• Simultaneous contrast • Interpretation of illumination
Shape (square, circle, etc.)	Physical shape of object	Viewing object at an angle	Taking slant into account
Size	Physical size of object	Viewing object at different distances	Taking distance into account.
Smell intensity	Amount of odorant	Increase strength of snif	Taking sniff strength into account

KEY TERMS: CHAPTER 6

Albedo. The percentage of light reflected from an object.

Chromatic adaptation. The adaptation of the eye to chromatic light.

Color constancy. The effect in which the perception of an object's hue remains constant even when the wavelength distribution of the illumination is changed. Approximate color constancy means that our perception of hue usually changes a little when the illumination changes, though not as much as we might expect from the change in the wavelengths of light reaching the eye.

Lightness constancy. The constancy of our perception of an object's lightness under different intensities of illumination.

Memory color. The idea that an object's characteristic color influences our perception of that object's color.

Penumbra. The fuzzy border at the edge of a shadow.

Perceptual constancy. The perception of a particular stimulus property, such as size, shape, or color, as remaining the same even when the conditions of stimulation are changed.

Ratio principle. A principle stating that two areas that reflect different amounts of light will look the same if the ratios of their intensities to the intensities of their surrounds are the same.

Shape constancy. The constancy of the perception of an object's shape that is maintained even when the object is viewed from different angles.

Size constancy. The constancy of the perception of the size of a stimulus that is maintained even when the object is viewed from different distances.

MULTIPLE CHOICE QUESTIONS

6.1 In the Uchihawa experiment, in which the light on the green color sample and the light adapting the subject we was viewing the sample were varied independently, color constancy was <u>worst</u> (the green paper's appearance was shifted towards the red), when the paper was illuminated with _____ and the subject was illuminated with _____. (3)
a) white; white
b) red; white
c) red; red

6.2 When lightness constancy is occurring, our perception of lightness is determined by (6)
a) our position relative to the illumination
b) the object's illumination
c) the object's albedo
d) the adaptation of the observer

6.3 The result of Gelb's experiment, in which a low-reflectance disc is illuminated by a hidden light, demonstrates (9)
a) lack of lightness constancy
b) lightness constancy

6.4 In the Mach card demonstration, in which a subject observes the lightness of the sides of a folded card before and after it perceptually flips, lightness constancy is influenced by (10)
a) the ratio of illumination on the two sides of the card
b) adaptation of the observer
c) lateral inhibition
d) interpretation of how an object is illuminated

6.5 According to Thouless, shape constancy is due to (15)
   a) taking the object's distance into account
   b) taking the object's orientation into account
   c) our past experience in seeing objects from
      different viewpoints
   d) lateral inhibition

6.6 There is a close relationship between the size of an
   object's image on the retina and our perception of the
   object's size (18)
   a) True
   b) False

6.7 Size constancy depends on (18)
   a) depth perception
   b) perception of the illumination
   c) knowledge of the sizes of familiar objects
   d) an object's distance relative to the observer

6.8 In which situation below does knowledge of the
   conditions of stimulation have no effect on perceptual
   constancy? (19)
   a) perceiving the shape of a Frisbee as a circle
   b) perceiving the distance and size of a nearby object
   c) perceiving the black disc as white in Gelb's
      "hidden light" demonstration.

CHAPTER 7

PERCEIVING OBJECTS

Like Chapter 6, this chapter analyzes perception from a behavioral perspective. This chapter looks at a number of ways that perception researchers have answered the question, "How do we perceive objects?" The main messages of the chapter are

1. Perception involves a process of perceptual organization in which different parts of a display are perceived as belonging together.

2. Object perception has been approached and explained in a number of different ways by different researchers.

3. Perception sometimes involves breaking a stimulus into its component parts and then reassembling these parts. This process occurs outside of consciousness.

CHAPTER ORGANIZATION

1. How objects in the environment are perceptually organized so we can tell one from another. This problem was studied by the Gestalt psychologists.

2. How neural processing results in object perception. This takes up where our discussion of extrastriate processing in Chapter 4 left off.

3. How stimuli are "perceptually processed" to result in object perception. This problem has been approached in a number of ways, all having in common the idea that perceptual processing involves (a) breaking stimuli down into basic components called "primitives," and (b) reassembling these primitives to create our perception of an object. The following three approaches hypothesize primitives: (1) feature integration, (2) computational, and (3) recognition by components.

4. How our knowledge of the world and the way the environment is constructed help us to perceive objects. This section introduces the idea that perception depends not only on the basic stimulus pattern (bottom-up processing) but also on what we bring to the perceptual situation because of our past history (top-down processing).

TABLE OF CONTENTS AND KEY TERMS

- pop-out boundary
- visual search
- illusory conjunctions

The Computational Approach
- computational approach
- raw primal sketch
- natural constraints
- 2-1/2-D sketch

Recognizing Objects: Determining What Things Are

The Recognition By Components Approach
- volumetric primitives
- recognition by components (RBC) approach
- geons
- view invariant
- principle of componential recovery

Knowledge, Experience & Processing

The Likelihood Principle And Hypothesis Testing
- likelihood principle
- hypothesis testing
- bottom-up processing
- top-down processing

Examples Of Top Down Processing

The Evolution Of Visual Processing
- neural plasticity

Something To Consider: Comparing The Ways Of Explaining Object Perception

Across The Senses: Shape Perception Through Vision And Touch.
- sensory substitution
- Optacon
- intersensory dominance

NOTES: CHAPTER 7

Comparing Approaches

This chapter describes a number of different ways that researchers have approached the study of object perception. Table 7.1 summarizes the approaches discussed in the chapter.

Table 7.1 Approaches to explaining object perception

Approach	Are There Primitives ?	Basic Principles
Gestalt (176)	No. The Gestalt approach is concerned with how the whole field is organized, not with what happens during early processing.	• Laws of organization • Wholes and parts • Figure-ground
Neural feature detectors (191)	Yes, neural primitives - the basic features that cause responses in single neurons.	• Feature detectors • Columnar organization • Distributed coding
Feature integration theory (195)	Yes, curvature, tilt, color, line ends, movement, closed areas, contrast, brightness.	• Preattentive processing • Free floating primitives • Focused attention stage

<u>Table 7.1</u> (Continued)

Approach	Are There Primitives ?	Basic Principles
Computational approach (199)	Yes, blobs, edge segments, bars, ends of edge segments.	• Raw primal sketch • 2-1/2 D sketch • Natural constraints
Recognition-by-components approach (203)	Yes, volumetric (3D) primitives called geons.	• Geons are view-invariant • Principle of componential recovery
Knowledge-based/cognitive approach (205)	No, the emphasis is on how prior knowledge affects perception.	• Likelihood principle • Hypothesis testing

KEY TERMS: CHAPTER 7

2 1/2-D sketch. The second stage of Marr's computational process. This stage is the result of processing the primitives. The resulting 2 1/2-D sketch is then transformed into the 3-D representation.

3-D representation. The end result of Marr's computational process; the perception of the three-dimensional stimulus.

Apparent movement (or stroboscopic movement). An illusion of movement that occurs between two objects separated in space when the objects are flashed rapidly on and off, one after another, separated by a brief time interval.

Bottom-up processing. Processing in which a person constructs a perception by first analyzing small units such as primitives. Treisman's preattentive stage of processing, in which a stimulus is analyzed into parts, is an example of bottom-up processing.

Common fate, law of. Gestalt law: Things that are moving in the same direction appear to be grouped together.

Componential recovery, principle of. A principle stating that, if an object's geons can be identified, then the object can be rapidly and correctly recognized.

Computational approach. An approach to explaining object perception that treats perception as the end result of a mathematical analysis of the retinal image.

Contrast. The difference in light intensity between two areas. For a visual grating stimulus, the contrast is the amplitude of the grating divided by its mean intensity.

Familiarity, law of. Gestalt law: Things are more likely to form groups if the groups appear familiar or meaningful.

Feature integration approach. The idea that object perception occurs through a sequence of steps that begins with the identification of basic features called primitives.

Feature integration theory. A sequence of steps proposed by Treisman to explain how objects are broken down into primitives and how these primitives are recombined to result in a perception of the object.

Focused-attention stage of processing. The stage of processing in which the primitives are combined. This stage requires conscious attention.

Geon. "Geometric ion"; Volumetric primitives proposed by Biederman.

Gestalt psychology. A school of psychology that has focused on developing principles of perceptual organization, proposing that "the whole is different from the sum of its parts."

Good continuation, law of. Gestalt law: Points that, when connected, result in straight or smoothly curving lines are seen as belonging together, and lines tend to be seen in such a way as to follow the smoothest path.

Good figure, law of. Gestalt law: Every stimulus pattern is seen so that the resulting structure is as simple as possible.

Ground The background that appears to extend behind the figure.

Hypothesis testing. The idea that sensory stimulation provides data for hypotheses about the world. According to this idea, perceiving involves testing different hypotheses about what is causing the stimulation.

Illusory conjunctions. Illusory combinations of primitives that are perceived when stimuli containing a number of primitives are presented briefly.

Illusory contours. Contours that are perceived even though they are not present in the physical stimulus.

Impossible object. An "object" that can be represented by a two-dimensional picture but cannot exist in three-dimensional space.

Interocular transfer. The aftereffect in one eye when an adaptation stimulus is presented to the other eye.

Intersensory dominance. When stimulation of one sense controls perception when placed in conflict with stimulation of another sense.

Laws of perceptual organization. See Perceptual organization, laws of.

Likelihood principle. A principle proposed by Helmholtz stating that we will perceive the object that is most likely to be the cause of our sensory stimulation.

Local depth information. Information at a localized place on a figure that indicates depth.

Natural constraints. Basic properties of the environment, such as the fact that intensity usually changes gradually at the borders of shadows. According to some theories of object perception, our perceptual system takes these properties into account as part of the process of object perception.

Neural plasticity. The fact that the anatomy and functionality of the nervous system can change in response to experience. Examples are how early visual experience can change the proportion of binocular neurons in the visual cortex, and how tactile experience can change the sizes of areas in the cortex that represent different parts of the body.

Optacon. A portable system that transforms printed letters or graphic images into patterns of vibration that can be sensed through the fingers.

Organization, laws of. See Perceptual organization, laws of.

Perceptual organization, laws of. Series of rules proposed by the Gestalt psychologists that specify how we organize small parts into wholes.

Perceptual organization. The perceptual grouping of small units into larger forms.

Perceptual processing. Mental or neural processing that occurs during the process of perception.

Pop-out boundaries. Boundaries between areas in a display that are seen almost immediately because they "pop out."

Pragnanz, law of. A gestalt law that is also called the law of good figure or the law of simplicity. It states that every stimulus pattern is seen in such a way that the resulting structure is as simple as possible.

Preattentive stage of processing. An automatic and rapid stage of processing, during which a stimulus is decomposed into small units called primitives.

Primitives. Basic stimuli which are the "building blocks" of more complex stimuli. For example, Treisman proposed primitives such as color, line tilt, and curvature. Biederman's primitives are volumetric shapes.

Principle of componential recovery. Biederman's principle stating that we can identify an object if we can perceive its individual geons.

Proximity, law of. Gestalt law: Things that are near to each other appear to be grouped together. Also called the law of nearness.

Raw Primal sketch. In Marr's computational approach to object perception, a rough sketch of the object that basically overlaps the light and dark areas of an image and which consists of an objects primitives and edges. The primal sketch occurs at an early stage of image processing and is not available to consciousness.

Recognition by components (RBC). A mechanism of object perception proposed by Biederman, in which we recognize objects by decomposing them into volumetric primitives called geons.

Reversible figure-ground. A figure-ground pattern that perceptually reverses as it is viewed, so that the figure becomes the ground and the ground becomes the figure.

Sensory substitution. Substituting one sense for the function served by another, as when touch is substituted for vision.

Similarity, law of. A Gestalt law stating that similar things appear to be grouped together.

Simplicity, law of. See Good figure, law of.

Structuralism. The approach to psychology, prominent in the late 19th and early 20th centuries, that postulated that perceptions result from the summation of many elementary sensations.

Subjective contour. See Illusory contour.

Texture segregation. The perceptual separation of fields with different textures.

View invariant. Shapes that have properties that don't change when viewed from different angles. The geons in the RBC theory of object perception are view invariant.

Visual form agnosia. A condition in which a person can see clearly but has difficulty recognizing what he or she sees. This condition, which is often caused by brain injuries, makes it difficult for people to synthesize parts of an object into an integrated whole.

Visual search. A procedure in which a subject's task is to find a particular element in a display that contains a number of elements.

Volumetric primitives. Primitives proposed in the recognition-by-components theory of recognition that are three-dimensional shapes that roughly correspond to an object's parts.

TEST YOURSELF

MULTIPLE CHOICE QUESTIONS

7.1   Perceptual organization is (1)
a) the way elements of a display are arranged on a page
b) organizing components of a scene to form perceptually separate objects
c) the sequence of steps that starts with the distal stimulus and culminates in perception
d) the way individual sensations interact to form perceptions

7.2   The main idea behind structuralism is that (4)
a) perception is determined by the addition of many elementary sensations
b) the whole is greater than the sum of its parts
c) the overall structure of an object determines the perception of that object
d) a "good figure" is one that is symmetrical and easily remembered

7.3   In the book, two dancers leaping together were used to illustrate the Gestalt law of (8)
a) simplicity
b) good continuation
c) figure and ground
d) common fate

7.4   Sometimes observing an object or a scene can cause us to change our interpretation of its identity (as in the forest-has-faces picture in the book). When this change occurs, it can be accompanied by a change in perceptual organization. (9)
a) True
b) False

7.5 When the regularities that usually occur in the
environment are violated, then   (12)
   a) we often misperceive what we see
   b) the Gestalt laws of organization can lead us to an
      incorrect interpretation of a scene
   c) we are usually not fooled into making incorrect
      perceptions
   d) a and b

7.6 Which of the following is <u>not</u> a property of figure and
ground? (13, 14)
   a) the contour separating figure and ground appears to
      be shared between the figure and the ground
   b) the figure is more memorable than the ground
   c) the figure is seen as being in front of the ground
   d) all of the above <u>are</u> properties of the figure and
      ground

7.7 In Weisstein and Wong's experiment, in which they
flashed vertical and slightly tilted lines onto
Rubin's face-vase reversible figure, subjects were
more accurate at judging line tilt when the line was
flashed on the area perceived as (18)
   a) ground
   b) figure

7.8 Which property below is <u>not</u> one of the properties that
are associated with neurons at higher levels in the
visual system? (21)
   a) neurons respond to more complex stimuli
   b) some neurons respond only to specific views of an
      object
   c) receptive fields get smaller
   d) some neurons respond to many views of an object

7.9 In Rolls and Tovee's experiment described in the text,
in which they recorded the response of neurons in the
monkey's IT cortex to a large number of face and non-
face stimuli, they found that   (24)
   a) most neurons responded to only 1-3 of the faces
   b) most neurons responded to faces but not to non
      faces
   c) most neurons responded to the two most potent
      biologically relevant stimuli: faces and food
   d) there was a substantial group of neurons that fired
      to pictures of food and scenes, but not to faces.

7.10 Which person below is most closely associated with the feature integration theory (FIT) of object perception? (26)
a) Ann Treisman
b) Irving Biederman
c) David Marr
d) Hermann von Helmholtz

7.11 According to the feature integration theory of object perception, primitives are detected during the _____ stage. (29)
a) preattentive
b) focused attention
c) 2-1/2 D sketch
d) 3-D representation

7.12 Which approach to form perception below does not involve primitives? (26, 37, 44)
a) Treisman: preattentive processing
b) Marr: computational approach
c) Biederman: recognition-by-components
d) all of the above involve primitives

7.13 According to Treisman (Feature Integration Theory), an important role of attention in perception is (34)
a) combining information in the ventral and dorsal processing streams
b) locating objects that are important to us
c) to isolate the primitives that are the building blocks of perception
d) to decide among competing perceptual hypotheses

7.14 Biederman (recognition-by-components) would explain our ability to identify an object that is partially hidden in terms of (46)
a) preattentive processing
b) the principle of componential recovery
c) focusing attention on specific locations
d) the principle of perceptual decomposition

7.15 Which is more dominant, when placed in conflict, vision or touch? (62)
a) vision
b) touch

CHAPTER 8

PERCEIVING VISUAL SPACE

This chapter is about how we perceive space, but the <u>main message</u> of the chapter has to do with the nature of <u>representation</u> in the visual system. How, we ask in this chapter, can information contained on a two-dimensional surface like the retina, indicate the depth we experience in the world? As we are answering this question, another message emerges: Perception often depends on multiple sources of information (a number of different depth cues in the case of depth perception).

CHAPTER ORGANIZATION

1. How information on the two-dimensional retinal surface indicates depth. A number of different types of depth cues are described, including cues that work with one eye (monocular) and a cue that requires two eyes (binocular). Most of the chapter is devoted to describing each of these cues and how they work. Since the binocular cue of disparity is the most complex, it is discussed in the most detail.

2. Physiology of binocular disparity. Here we return to the physiological approach of Chapters 2 - 4, looking at the physiology of binocular vision in two ways:

    (a) Describing the properties of binocular depth cells, that respond selectively to specific amounts of binocular disparity.

    (b) Describing the development of binocular vision by looking at the results of experiments in which animals are deprived of vision in one eye as they are growing up. The results of these experiments show that early binocular experience is important for the development of depth perception. These results can also be generalized to humans.

TABLE OF CONTENTS AND KEY TERMS

NOTES: CHAPTER 8

Binocular Disparity and Stereopsis (222)

Binocular disparity and stereopsis are often confused. This confusion is an example of how physical and perceptual, a distinction we described at the end of Chapter 2, are often confused.

Binocular disparity is <u>physical</u> - it refers to where the images of an object fall on the left and right eyes. But just because two images fall on disparate (non corresponding) points, this doesn't mean depth perception will result. For example, if an animal is reared so it can see out of only one eye when it is young, it will grow up without binocular cells. For this organism, images that fall on disparate points still result in disparity, but will not result in depth perception.

Stereopsis is the perception of depth that results from disparity, and is therefore <u>perceptual</u>. Binocular disparity and stereopsis are, therefore, closely related, but are not the same thing.

The Horopter (227)

The horopter is the imaginary curved surface that passes through the point of fixation, and which defines the location of points that will create images that fall on corresponding points. It is important to realize, however, that the horopter changes anytime we change where we look. The key thing to realize is that the horopter always passes through the point of fixation. Thus, every time you change your fixation (which can happen up to three times a second), a new horopter is created, and this new horopter defines a new family of locations that result in images on corresponding points.

KEY TERMS: CHAPTER 8

Accommodation (depth cue). A depth cue. Muscular sensations that occur when the eye accommodates to bring objects at different distances into focus may provide information regarding the distance of that object.

Accretion. The uncovering of the farther of two surfaces due to observer movement.

Aerial perspective. See Atmospheric perspective.

Alberti's window. A transparent surface on which an artist traces the scene viewed through the surface in order to draw a picture in linear perspective.

Amblyopia. A large reduction in the acuity in one eye.

Angle of disparity. The visual angle between the images of an object on the two retinas. If the images of an object fall on corresponding points, the angle of disparity is zero. If the images fall on noncorresponding points, the angle of disparity indicates the degree of noncorrespondence.

Atmospheric perspective. A depth cue. Objects that are farther away look more blurred and bluer than objects that are closer, because we must look through more air and particles to see them.

Binocular deprivation. Depriving an animal of vision in one eye during some portion of their development.

Binocular depth cell. A neuron in the visual cortex that responds best to stimuli that fall on points separated by a specific degree of disparity on the two retinas.

Binocular depth cue. A depth cue that requires the participation of both eyes. Binocular disparity is the major binocular depth cue.

Binocular disparity. The result when the retinal images of an object fall on disparate points on the two retinas.

Convergence (depth cue). A depth cue. Muscular sensations that occur when the eyes move inward (convergence) or outward (divergence) to view objects at different distances may provide information regarding the depth of that object.

Convergence angle. The angle between the two eyes as they fixate on an object.

Correspondence problem. The visual system's matching of points on one image with similar points on the other image in order to determine binocular disparity.

Corresponding retinal points. The points on each retina that would overlap if one retina were slid on top of the other. Receptors at corresponding points send their signals to the same locations in the brain.

Crossed disparity. Binocular disparity in which objects are located in front of the horopter. (See uncrossed disparity)

Cue theory. The approach to depth perception that focuses on identifying information in the retinal image that is correlated with depth in the world.

Deletion. The covering of the farther of two surfaces due to observer movement. This provides information for depth.

Depth cues. Two-dimensional information on the retina that is correlated with depth in the scene.

Direct perception. J. J. Gibson's idea that we pick up the information provided by invariants directly and that perceptions result from this information without the need of any further processing.

Disparate points. See Noncorresponding points.

Disparity detectors. Neurons that respond best to stimuli that fall on retinal point separated by a specific angle of disparity. Also called binocular depth cells.

Echolocation. Locating objects by sending out high-frequency pulses and sensing the echo created when these pulses are reflected from objects in the environment. Echolocation is used by bats and dolphins.

Emmert's law. A law stating that the size of an afterimage depends on the distance of the surface against which the afterimage is viewed. The farther away the surface against which an afterimage is viewed, the larger the afterimage appears.

Familiar size. A depth cue. Our knowledge of an object's actual size sometimes influences our perception of an object's distance.

Fourier spectrum. The sine-wave components that make up a periodic waveform. Fourier spectra are usually depicted by a line for each sine-wave frequency, the height of the line indicating the amount of energy at that frequency.

Frontal eyes. Eyes located in front of the head, so the views of the two eyes overlap.

Horopter. An imaginary surface that passes through the point of fixation. Objects falling on this surface result in images that fall on corresponding points on the two retinas.

Interocular transfer. The aftereffect in one eye when an adaptation stimulus is presented to the other eye.

Lateral eyes. Eyes located on opposite sides of an animal's head, so the views of the two eyes do not overlap or overlap only slightly, as in the pigeon and the rabbit.

Linear perspective (depth cue). The visual effect that parallel lines (like railroad tracks) converge as they get farther away. This convergence of parallel lines is a depth cue, with greater convergence indicating greater distance.

Linear perspective (drawing system). A method of representing three-dimensional space on a two-dimensional surface.

Monocular depth cues. Depth cues, such as overlap, relative size, relative height, familiar size, linear perspective, movement parallax, and accommodation that work if we use only one eye.

Monocular rearing. Rearing an animal so it has use of only one eye. When done at a young age this rearing affects development of binocular neurons in the cortex.

Motion parallax. A depth cue. As an observer moves, nearby objects appear to move rapidly whereas far objects appear to move slowly.

Movement-produced cues. Cues that create the impression of depth from movement. The movement-produced cues are motion parallax and deletion and accretion.

Noncorresponding (disparate) points. Two points, one on each retina, that would not overlap if the retinas were slid onto each other.

Occlusion. Depth cue in which one object hides or partially hides another object from view, causing the hidden object to be perceived as being farther away.

Ocular dominance histogram. A histogram that indicates the degree of ocular dominance of a large population of neurons.

Oculomotor cues. Depth cues that depend on our ability to sense the position of our eyes and the tension in our eye muscles. Accommodation and convergence are oculomotor cues.

Overlap. A depth cue. If object A covers object B, then object A is seen as being in front of object B.

Pictorial cues. Depth cues, such as overlap, relative height, and relative size, that can be depicted in pictures.

Random-dot stereogram. A stereogram in which the stimuli are pictures of random dots. If one section of this pattern is shifted slightly in one direction, the resulting disparity causes the perception of depth when the patterns are viewed in a stereoscope.

Rayleigh scattering. The scattering of sunlight by small particles in the earth's atmosphere, the amount of scatter being inversely proportional to the fourth power of the light's wavelength. Thus, short-wavelength light is scattered more than long-wavelength light and this is why we see the sky as blue.

Relative height. A depth cue. Objects that have bases below the horizon appear to be farther away if they are higher in the field of view. If the object's bases are above the horizon, they appear to be farther away if they are lower in the field of view.

Relative size. A cue for depth perception. If two objects are of equal size, the one that is farther away will take up less of the field of view.

Retinal size. The size of an image on the retina.

Sensitive period. A period of time, usually early in an organism's life, during which changes in the environment have a large effect on the organism's physiology or behavior.

Stereopsis. The impression of depth that results from differences in the images on the retinas of the two eyes.

Stereoscope. A device that presents pictures to the left and the right eyes so that the binocular disparity a person would experience when viewing an actual scene is duplicated. The result is a convincing illusion of depth.

Stimulus deprivation amblyopia. Amblyopia due to early closure of one eye.

Strabismus. A condition in which an imbalance in the eye muscles upsets the coordination between the two eyes.

Texture gradient. The pattern formed by a regularly textured surface that extends away from the observer. The elements in a texture gradient appear smaller as distance from the observer increases.

Tilt aftereffect. The result when staring at an adapting field of tilted lines and then looking at vertical lines causes the vertical lines to appear to be tilted in a direction opposite to the tilt of the adapting field.

Uncrossed disparity. Binocular disparity that occurs when objects are located beyond the horopter. (See Crossed disparity)

Ventriloquism effect. See Visual capture.

Visual capture. When sound is heard coming from its seen location, even though it is actually originating somewhere else. Also called the ventriloquism effect.

TEST YOURSELF

MULTIPLE CHOICE QUESTIONS

8.1 The depth cue of convergence (3)
   a) involves a bulging of the lens
   b) involves the muscles of the eye
   c) is effective only at distances greater than about
      10 feet from the observer
   d) involves a comparison of the images in the left and
      right eyes

8.2 Which of the following go together (4)
   a) pictorial cue- monocular cue
   b) disparity - pictorial cue
   c) motion parallax - binocular disparity
   d) movement-produced cue- binocular cue

8.3 Alberti's window is associated with (5)
   a) texture gradients
   b) motion parallax
   c) linear perspective
   d) height in the field of view

8.4 The stereoscope is most closely associated with (8)
   a) atmospheric perspective
   b) binocular disparity
   c) linear perspective
   d) convergence

8.5 Stereopsis is (9)
   a) the same thing as disparity
   b) the perception of depth created from disparity
   c) depth perception caused by oculomotor cues
   d) closely associated with linear perspective

8.6 Crossed disparity occurs when objects are located (13)
   a) on the horopter
   b) beyond the horopter
   c) in front of the horopter

8.7 The visual system can calculate an object's disparity only if it can compare the two images in the left and right eyes. This creates a problem called the _____ problem. (15)
a) correspondence
b) matching
c) stereopsis
d) disparity

8.8 Which depth cue below is effective over the greatest range of distances? (16)
a) motion
b) disparity
c) atmospheric perspective
d) relative size

8.9 A binocular depth cell will not respond (17)
a) to moving stimuli
b) when disparate points on the two eyes are stimulated
c) when only one eye is stimulated
d) when both eyes are stimulated simultaneously

8.10 A binocular depth cell can be tuned to respond to zero disparity (19)
a) True
b) False

8.11 The sensitive period for causing changes in the cat's visual system by means of monocular deprivation is (24)
a) between birth and 3 weeks of age
b) between 4 weeks and 6 months of age
c) between 6 and 10 months of age

8.12 Amblyopia refers to a condition in which (28)
a) a person sees vertical shapes clearly but sees horizontals out of focus
b) one eye has much lower acuity than the other eye
c) vision is fogged due to a clouding of the lens
d) a person's eye muscles are out of balance

8.13 _____ eyes are best suited for using binocular disparity for depth perception. (31)
   a) lateral
   b) frontal

8.14 Bats experience an "acoustic scene" (36)
   a) in the same way that humans experience a visual scene
   b) as a series of pulses with different durations
   c) as the firing of groups of neurons with different "best delays"
   d) we can't answer this question since we have no way of knowing about what a bat experiences.

8.15 When we hear a sound as coming from its <u>seen</u> location rather than from another location, where it is actually produced, this is called (39)
   a) the auditory space error
   b) echolocation
   c) visual capture
   d) the auditory-visual space paradox

CHAPTER 9:

SIZE, ILLUSIONS, AND ECOLOGICAL
ASPECTS OF PERCEPTION

The main topic of this chapter is how the perception of size is related to the perception of depth. And since many of the visual illusions are illusions that cause us to misperceive size, the topic of size perception naturally leads into a discussion of visual illusions. This chapter is also about the ecology of perception, including J. J. Gibson's ideas on how perception works.

CHAPTER ORGANIZATION

1. The information we use to perceive size and which causes size constancy to occur.

2.. Some common visual illusions (focusing on ones that involve size perception) and what causes them.

3. Some examples of how perception has evolved to best serve the needs of different animals.

4. How J. J. Gibson's ecological approach explains perception. Gibson's approach focuses on determining how people use information under natural environmental conditions.

TABLE OF CONTENTS AND KEY TERMS

NOTES: CHAPTER 9

<u>Perceiving Size</u> (246)

One way to understand size perception is to think of the visual system as starting with an object's visual angle (or retinal size, since these two things are directly related to one another) and then taking its perceived distance into account. The following rules follow from this idea:

(1) <u>Rule 1</u>: If two objects have the same visual angle, the one that appears farther away will appear larger. This is illustrated by the results of Holway and Boring's experiment (Figure 9.4), in which all stimuli were one degree in visual angle and the farther ones appeared larger. Note that when depth cues were eliminated in this experiment, so all of the stimuli appeared to be at the same distance, then all of the stimuli appeared to be the same size. Thus, a corollary to the above "rule" is that if two objects have the same visual angle and appear to be at the same distance, then they will appear equal in size.

(2) <u>Rule 2</u>: If two objects appear the same distance, the one with the larger visual angle will appear larger. This is the situation in the Ames room (Figure 9.17) in which both people appear to be a the same distance, so the one on the right, with the larger visual angle, appears larger. This example illustrates the importance of the word <u>appears</u> in our rules. The perception of size depends on the <u>perceived</u> distance, not the real physical distance. The reason the Ames room works is that even though the two people are a different distances they <u>appear</u> to be at the same distance.

<u>The Moon Illusion</u> (256)

It has been said that the existence of a large number of explanations for a phenomenon means that we don't yet understand it. The moon illusion is an example of such a situation. A number of explanations have been proposed, but which explanation is correct is still a matter of controversy among perception researchers.

The apparent distance theory was, until recently, the theory favored by most researchers. This theory is based on Rule #1 above that if two objects have the same visual angle, the one that appears farther away will appear larger. We can see that this is so from Figure 9.5 in the text, which shows three stimuli with the same visual angle. From this example, it is obvious that the stimuli that are farther away are larger and will, therefore, be perceived as larger.

The apparent distance theory starts with this observation and then proposes that the horizon moon appears larger because it appears farther away. Students sometimes have a problem accepting this idea since they say that the horizon moon appears closer because it appears larger. A proponent of the apparent distance theory would probably answer this statement by saying that focusing on the size of the moon (which is what we are trying to explain) confuses the issue, and that the real perceived distance of the horizon moon is more accurately represented by the "flattened heavens" observation shown in Figure 9.20. Proponents of another theory, the angular size contrast theory, say that the illusion is caused not by apparent depth, but by a comparison process in which the angular size of the moon is compared to its surroundings. These two theories are summarized in Table 9.1 below:

<u>Table 9.1</u> Two Theories of the Moon Illusion.

Theory	Key Factor	Example	Evidence
Apparent distance theory	Apparent distance of the moon	The horizon moon appears farther away, so size-distance scaling causes it to appear larger.	• Moon appears larger over far horizons • People report that the heavens appear flattened, with the horizon farther away.
Angular size-contrast theory	Size of surrounding objects	Elevated moon appears smaller because it is surrounded by a large object (the expanse of sky).	• Objects like buildings are smaller on the far horizon, which explains why the moon appears larger when seen against far horizons.

<u>Invariant Information</u> (262)

Invariant information is one of those concepts that sounds complex, but is really quite simple. The key is the word "invariant," which can be roughly translated as "unchanging" or "constant."

The reason the idea of invariant information is so powerful is that one of the basic properties of perception is that we are moving most of the time, and even when we are sitting still, our eyes are moving. This constant movement causes changes in the image on our retina, yet we tend to see the world as stable and the properties of objects as constant (see perceptual constancy, Chapter 6). Invariant information is information that remains constant in spite of the changes that occur in the retinal image. The classic example, illustrated in Figures 9.25 is the texture gradient.

Imagine that you are standing on a huge checkerboard that extends into the distance. This checkerboard creates a texture gradient, with the squares appearing to get smaller and more closely spaced as they extend into the distance. This texture provides information that you can use to judge depth and size, and the information is invariant - no matter where you look on this huge checkerboard, the texture gradient is there, and this situation continues to hold even if you walk to another location on the checkerboard. According to J. J. Gibson's ecological approach to perception, much of our perception is determined by invariant information.

KEY TERMS: CHAPTER 9

Ames room. A distorted room, first built by Adelbert Ames, that creates an erroneous perception of the sizes of people in the room. The room is constructed so that two people at the far wall of the room appear to stand at the same distance from an observer. In actuality, one of the people is much farther away than the other.

Angular size-contrast theory. An explanation of the moon illusion that states that the perceived size of the moon is determined by the sizes of the objects that surround it. According to this idea, the moon appears small when it is surrounded by large objects, such as the expanse of the sky when the moon is overhead.

Apparent distance theory. An explanation of the moon illusion that is based on the idea that the horizon moon, which is viewed across the filled space of the terrain, should appear farther away than the zenith moon, which is viewed through the empty space of the sky. This theory states that, since the horizon and zenith moons have the same visual angle, the farther-appearing horizon moon should appear larger.

Area centralis. The horizontal area of high receptor density found in some animals, such as the turtle.

Conflicting cues theory. A theory of visual illusions proposed by R. H. Day, which states that our perception of the length of lines depends on an integration the actual length of lines and the overall length of the figure.

Ecological approach. The approach to perception that emphasizes studying perception as it occurs in natural settings, particularly emphasizing the role of observer movement.

Emmert's law. A law stating that the size of an afterimage depends on the distance of the surface against which the afterimage is viewed. The farther away the surface against which an afterimage is viewed, the larger the afterimage appears.

Gradient of flow. In a flow pattern a gradient is created by movement of an observer through the environment. The speed of movement is rapid in the foreground and becomes slower as distance from the observer increases.

132

Horizon ratio principle. A principle stating that, if a person is standing on flat terrain, a point on an object that intersects the horizon will be one eye-height above the ground, and that if two objects that are in contact with the ground are the same size, the proportions of the objects above and below the horizon will be the same.

Horizon ratio. The proportion of an object that is above the horizon divided by the proportion that is below the horizon.

Illusion. A situation in which an observer's perception of a stimulus does not correspond to the physical properties of the stimulus. For example, in the Muller-Lyer illusion, two lines of equal length are perceived to be of different lengths.

Invariant information. Environmental properties that do not change as the observer moves. For example, the spacing, or texture, of the elements in a texture gradient does not change as the observer moves on the gradient. The texture of the gradient therefore supplies invariant information for depth perception.

Misapplied size constancy scaling. A principle, proposed by Gregory, that when mechanisms that help maintain size constancy in the three-dimensional world are applied to two-dimensional pictures, an illusion of size sometimes results.

Moon illusion. An illusion in which the moon appears to be larger when it is on or near the horizon than when it is high in the sky.

Muller-Lyer illusion. An illusion consisting of two lines of equal length that appear to be different lengths because of the addition of "fins" to the ends of the lines.

Optic array. The way the light of the environment is structured by the presence of objects, surfaces, and textures.

Ponzo illusion. An illusion of size in which two rectangles of equal length that are drawn between two converging lines appear to be different in length. Also called the railroad track illusion.

Size constancy. The constancy of the perception of the size of a stimulus that is maintained even when the object is viewed from different distances.

Size cues. Cues such as familiar size and relative size that help us determine the sizes of objects.

Size-distance scaling. A hypothesized mechanism that helps maintain size constancy by taking an object's distance into account.

Texture gradient. The pattern formed by a regularly textured surface that extends away from the observer. The elements in a texture gradient appear smaller as distance from the observer increases.

Veridical perception. Perception that matches the actual physical situation.

Visual angle. The angle between two lines that extend from the observer's eye, one line extending to one end of an object and the second to the other end of the object. An object's visual angle is always determined relative to an observer; therefore, an object's visual angle changes as the distance between the object and the observer changes.

MULTIPLE CHOICE QUESTIONS

9.1 Knowing the size of an object enables us to determine the object's visual angle. (1, 2)
a) True
b) False

9.2 In Holway and Boring's size perception experiment all of the test stimuli (5)
a) were the same size
b) increased in visual angle as their distances down the hallway increased
c) appeared to be different sizes when depth cues were eliminated
d) appeared to be the same size when depth cues were eliminated

9.3 Holway and Boring found that (5, 6)
a) size constancy holds under all conditions
b) the law of visual angle does not work for humans
c) the law of visual angle holds only if depth cues are present
d) if depth cues are present size constancy holds

9.4 Emmert's law states that (10)
a) our perception of size depends on the presence of depth information
b) afterimages that are perceived as farther away are perceived as smaller
c) the size of an afterimage depends on the distance of the afterimage
d) b and c

9.5 Veridical perception is (11)
a) perception that is in error
b) perception that matches the actual physical situation
c) perception in which a shift towards the vertical occurs
d) the idea that we can't really describe our own private perceptions in words

9.6 According to Gregory, the upper horizontal rectangle in the Ponzo (railroad track) illusion looks larger than the lower one because (12)
a) of voluntary eye movements
b) of Emmert's law
c) the retinal size of the upper rectangle is larger
d) of size-distance scaling

9.7 Which of the following explanations of the Muller-Lyer illusion focuses on length as a key variable? (14)
a) misapplied size constancy scaling
b) angular size-contrast theory
c) conflicting cues theory
d) distance averaging theory

9.8 The horizon moon has _____ the moon that is elevated in the sky. (18)
a) the same visual angle as
b) a larger visual angle than
c) a smaller visual angle than

9.9 Emmert's law is most closely related to the _____ theory of the moon illusion. (19)
a) angular size-contrast
b) apparent distance
c) ecological
d) upward gaze

9.10 Which of the following illusions is not an example of an illusion that is influenced by context? (22)
a) Ponzo illusion
b) Muller-Lyer illusion
c) Ames room
d) none of the above (they are all influenced by context

9.11 Who below is most closely associated with the ecological approach to perception? (25, c)
a) Richard Gregory
b) Adelbert Ames
c) J. J. Gibson
d) Kaufman and Rock

9.12 Which of the following is <u>least</u> associated with the ecological approach to perception? (26, a)
a) depth cues
b) the horizon ratio
c) direct perception
d) texture gradients

9.13 When Gibson says that perception is <u>direct</u> he means that (30, d)
a) it is a direct outcome of taking factors that influence perception, such as distance, into account.
b) it is a result of physiological processes that directly affect perception
c) it is the result of calculations that directly lead to perception
d) it is the result of information taken directly from the optic array

9.14 According to the _____ approach to perception, we perceive the sizes of the people in the Ames room by taking retinal size and perceived distance into account. (32, b)
a) direct
b) processing
c) veridical
d) cue

9.15 Which of the following is <u>not</u> a similarity that has been observed between the visual and haptic versions of illusions? (38, d)
a) the size of the effect is similar
b) both decrease in a similar way over many trials
c) there is cross-adaptation between them (presenting visual stimuli can affect the haptic version, for example)
d) both take a few trials to reach maximum size

CHAPTER 10

PERCEIVING MOVEMENT

This chapter, which is the last one to consider visual perception, illustrates two approaches to studying a perceptual quality: (1) Asking what causes us to perceive that perceptual quality. For example, we can ask what is it about the stimuli and neural responding that results in the perception of motion; (2) Asking what role a particular perceptual quality plays in perceiving other qualities. For example, we can ask how movement perception helps us to perceive shape. This chapter includes both of these approaches to studying movement perception.

This chapter also considers what kinds of information are important for movement perception. We see that just looking at what's happening on the retina isn't enough, because we can sometimes perceive movement when there is no movement on the retina, and we can sometimes perceive no movement when there is movement on the retina.

CHAPTER ORGANIZATION

1. What perceiving movement tells us about the world.

2. How we can explain movement perception on the basis of neural firing. This discussion builds on our discussion about neural circuits in Chapter 2 and modularity in Chapter 4.

3. How we can deal with the fact that we can perceive movement even when there is no stimulus movement on the retina, such as when a person follows a moving stimulus with their eyes. One way of dealing with this problem involves a hypothetical mechanism called the corollary discharge. Another way is by considering how stimuli in the environment move relative to one another.

4. How movement perception is influenced by the context within which stimuli move.

5. How movement provides information about the world that enables us to (a) perceive shape and organization; (b) negotiate our way through the environment, and (c) maintain our balance.

139

TABLE OF CONTENTS AND KEY TERMS

140

NOTES: CHAPTER 10

Corollary Discharge Theory (284)

The corollary discharge model of motion perception hypothesizes that we will perceive motion when a corollary discharge signal (generated when a signal to move the eyes is sent to the eye muscles) reaches a structure called the comparator, which then sends a signal to the brain, or if an image movement signal (generated when an image moves across the retina) reaches the comparator. If, however, both of these signals reach the comparator simultaneously, they cancel each other, the comparator sends no signal to the brain, and no movement is perceived.

One way this model has been tested is to set up situations in which only the corollary discharge reaches the comparator. The model predicts that the observer should perceive movement in that situation, and this is, in fact, what happens. Table 10.1 summarizes the four ways that this has been achieved. Note that in each of these cases there is a corollary discharge signal and no image movement signal, so movement is perceived.

Table 10.1 Four ways to generate a corollary discharge signal without generating an image movement signal (285)

Condition	Eye moves?	Retinal Image Moves?	Corollary Discharge?
View afterimage while the eyes are moving in the dark	Yes	No. The after-image is caused by an area of bleached pigment on the retina.	Yes. A signal is sent to move the eyes.
Push on the side of the eyeball while looking at a stationary point	No	No. The observer is looking steadily at one spot.	Yes. A signal is sent to the eye muscles to counteract the push on the eyeball and keep the eye stationary.
Follow a moving object with eyes	Yes	No. The image of the followed object stays on the fovea.	Yes. A signal is sent to the eyes to cause eye movements.
A subject with paralyzed eye muscles tries to move the eye	No	No. The eye is paralyzed, so it can't move.	Yes. A signal is sent to the eyes to try to move them.

Angular expansion, rate of. The rate at which a moving object's visual angle expands as it gets closer to an observer.

Apparent movement (or stroboscopic movement). An illusion of movement that occurs between two objects separated in space when the objects are flashed rapidly on and off, one after another, separated by a brief time interval. (7, 10)

Biological movement. Motion produced by biological organisms. Most of the experiments on biological motion have used walking humans with lights attached to their joints and limbs as stimuli.

Comparator. A structure hypothesized by the corollary discharge theory of movement perception. The corollary discharge signal and the sensory movement signal meet at the comparator.

Corollary discharge signal (CDS). A copy of the signal sent from the motor area of the brain to the eye muscles. The corollary discharge signal is sent not to the eye muscles, but to the hypothetical comparator of corollary discharge theory.

Corollary discharge theory. According to the corollary discharge theory of motion perception, the corollary discharge signal is sent to a structure called the comparator, where the information in the corollary discharge is compared to the sensory movement signal. If the corollary discharge signal and the sensory movement signal do not cancel each other, movement is perceived.

Flow pattern. Pattern of visual stimulation that is created as elements in the environment flow past an observer due to observer motion.

Focus of expansion (F. O. E.) The point in the flow pattern caused by observer movement in which there is no expansion. According to Gibson, the focus of expansion always remains centered on the observer's destination.

Global optical flow. Information for movement that occurs when all elements in a scene move.

Illusions of movement. The perception of movement in situations in which there is actually no movement in the physical stimulus. Examples of illusions of movement are the waterfall illusion, induced movement, and stroboscopic movement.

Image movement signal. In corollary discharge theory, the signal that occurs when an image stimulates the receptors by moving across them.

Induced movement. The illusory movement of one object that is caused by the movement of another object that is nearby.

Interstimulus interval (ISI). The time interval between two flashes of light in an apparent movement display.

Kinetic depth effect. The resulting effect when a stimulus's three-dimensional structure becomes apparent from viewing a two-dimensional image of the stimulus as it rotates.

Local movement signal. Information for movement that occurs when one object moves in an otherwise stationary field.

Locomotor flow line. The flow line that passes directly under a moving observer.

Motion agnosia. An effect of brain damage in which the ability to perceive motion is disrupted.

Motor signal. In corollary discharge theory, the signal that is sent to the eye muscles when the observer moves or tries to move his or her eyes.

Movement aftereffect. An illusion of movement that occurs after a person views an inducing stimulus such as a waterfall.

Optic flow pattern. The flow pattern that occurs when an observer moves relative to the environment. Forward movement causes an expanding optic flow pattern, whereas backward movement causes a contracting optic flow pattern. The term optic flow field is used by some researchers to refer to this flow pattern.

Rate of angular expansion. See Angular expansion, rate of.

Real movement. The physical movement of a stimulus.

Real movement neuron. Type of neuron in area V3 that responds when stimulus movement across the retina is caused by movement of the stimulus but does not respond if stimulus movement on the retina is caused by movement of the eyes.

Sensory movement signal. The electrical signal generated by the movement of an image across the retina. This is one of the signals that plays a role in the corollary discharge theory of movement perception.

Shortest-path constraint. The principle that apparent movement occurs along the shortest path between two stimuli that cause apparent movement when flashed on and off with the appropriate timing.

Stroboscopic movement. See Apparent movement.

Waterfall illusion. An aftereffect of movement that occurs after viewing a stimulus moving in one direction, such as a waterfall. Viewing the waterfall creates an illusion of movement of other objects in the opposite direction.

MULTIPLE CHOICE QUESTIONS

10.1 A pigeon's head appears to move backwards when its body moves forward. This is an example of (2)
   a) the effect of past experience on movement perception
   b) stroboscopic movement
   c) a movement aftereffect
   d) induced movement

10.2 There are a number of situations in which images remain stationary on the retina, but we perceive movement. Which of the following is an example of this? (4)
   a) walking through the environment.
   b) the waterfall illusion
   c) induced movement
   d) b and c

10.3 Decreasing the interstimulus interval between two flashes of light always increases the apparent movement effect (8)
   a) True
   b) False

10.4 The earliest place in the visual system where directionally selective neurons are found is (10)
   a) the striate cortex
   b) the lateral geniculate nucleus
   c) the medial temporal area (MT)
   d) the inferotemporal cortex (IT)

10.5 The direction a stimulus is moving cannot be accurately determined by monitoring the firing of complex cortical cells that are tuned to respond best to a specific direction of movement, because (13)
   a) stimulus intensity influences the cell's firing
   b) the cell fires to more than one direction of movement
   c) the cells' firing rate is influenced by the velocity that the stimulus is moving.
   d) all of the above

10.6 The results of Newsome's experiments in which monkey's observed moving dot patterns, show that the direction of movement can be determined by the activity of _____ neurons in MT cortex. (16)
a) a small number of
b) a large population of

10.7 According to corollary discharge theory, when we track a moving car with our eyes (17, 21)
a) a sensory movement signal is generated by the car
b) a corollary discharge signal is generated by movement of the eyes and a sensory movement signal is generated by movement of the image of the background
c) the corollary discharge is canceled by the sensory movement signal from the car
d) only a corollary discharge is generated

10.7 The corollary discharge signal occurs when (18)
a) an image moves across the retina
b) the eye moves
c) a signal is sent to the eye to move it
d) movement is actually perceived

10.8 Pushing on the eyeball while keeping the eye fixated on a stationary spot causes a corollary discharge signal (21)
a) True
b) False

10.10 A real movement neuron is one that responds (22)
a) any time a stimulus moves across a receptive field
b) to the movement of real environmental stimuli, such as people walking
c) only to a bar that is really moving in space
d) when movement on the retina occurs because of eye movements

10.11 Experiments described in the text in which pictures of a person with their arms in different positions are flashed, show that (28, 29)
a) the shortest-path constraint holds under all conditions
b) it takes time for the visual system to process information about complex meaningful stimuli
c) there is really nothing special about meaningful stimuli when it comes to perceiving apparent movement
d) real movement of the arms is more convincing than apparent movement

10.12 Transforming a two-dimensional image into a three-dimensional perception is most closely associated with (31)
a) apparent motion
b) the kinetic depth effect
c) biological motion
d) the correspondence problem

10.13 According to Gibson, the crucial source of information for reaching our destination is (35)
a) the locomotor flow line
b) the shortest path constraint
c) the focus of expansion
d) the estimated time of arrival

10.14 _____ is associated with the locomotor flow line. (37)
a) The idea that vision is a proprioceptive sense
b) Lee's swinging room experiments
c) Movement parallax
d) Driving on the highway

10.15 When we say that vision is a proprioceptive sense, we are saying that vision plays a role in the perception of (40)
a) body movement
b) stimulus structure
c) shape by active touch
d) movement

CHAPTER 11:

SOUND, THE AUDITORY SYSTEM, AND PITCH PERCEPTION

This chapter introduces the science of hearing and so provides the challenge of learning about new stimuli, structures, and anatomy. You will see that the auditory system differs from the visual system in a number of ways, but that many of the principles you became familiar with in studying vision also play important roles in the process of hearing.

CHAPTER ORGANIZATION

1. The functions of hearing in our lives.

2. How we describe and measure the physical characteristics of sound.

3. The perceptual outcomes of the sound stimulus, emphasizing the difference between the physical and perceptual that was highlighted in some of the chapters on vision.

4. The key structures of the auditory system, how they are connected, and how they respond to the sound stimulus.

5. The sensory code for pitch, emphasizing the place theory of pitch perception, as outlined by Georg von Bekesy, and the timing code for pitch perception. This section is the most important part of the chapter (but you need to know what came before it in order to understand it!), because it shows how both behavioral and physiological evidence have been important in deducing the sensory code for pitch.

6. The following additional phenomena that go beyond place and timing: (1) periodicity pitch, (2) complex auditory stimuli, and (3) parallel pathways

TABLE OF CONTENTS AND KEY TERMS

Auditory System: Structure And Function (318)

The Outer Ear

- outer ear
- pinna
- auditory canal
- tympanic membrane
- ear drum
- resonance
- resonant frequency

The Middle Ear

- middle ear
- ossicles
- malleus
- incus
- stapes
- oval window
- middle ear muscles

The Inner Ear

- inner ear
- cochlea
- cochlear partition
- organ of Corti
- basilar membrane
- tectorial membrane
- hair cells
- inner hair cells
- outer hair cells
- cilia
- round window

The Auditory Pathways

- cochlear nucleus
- superior olivary nucleus
- inferior colliculus
- medial geniculate nucleus
- auditory receiving area
- secondary auditory cortex

NOTES: CHAPTER 11

Organ of Corti

What is the organ of Corti and how does it operate? This is often confusing because of the complexity of the structure and the structures that surround it.

The organ of Corti is the structure that contains the inner and outer hair cells. It is situated between two membranes, which are often confused. As shown in Figures 11.17 and 11.19, the basilar membrane is on the bottom (remember that basilar and bottom both start with "b.") and the tectorial membrane is on the top (tectorial membrane and top both start with "t.").

The function of the basilar membrane is to vibrate with a traveling wave in response to the sound stimulus. Since the organ of Corti is sitting on top of the basilar membrane it vibrates as well. One function of the tectorial membrane is to bend the outer hair cells. This occurs when the organ of Corti and the tectorial membrane move in response to the sound stimulus. Since the tips of the outer hair cells are in contact with the tectorial membrane. The movement of both of them causes the hair cells to bend. Remember that the basilar membrane creates the vibration of the organ of Corti and the tectorial membrane helps bend the outer hair cells.

The Envelope of the Traveling Wave (327)

The basilar membrane vibrates with a traveling wave motion in response to the sound stimulus, and the envelope of the traveling wave is the line that connects the points of maximum displacement of the basilar membrane. Even after reading this definition, many people are still left wondering exactly what the traveling wave is.

One way to understand what the traveling wave is, is to look at another complex motion - the path that a basketball takes as a player dribbles the ball down court. The player starts with small rapid dribbles and then changes to larger more spaced out dribbles as he runs down the court. If we were to draw a picture of the path taken by the basketball, it might look something like the curve on the left on the next page.

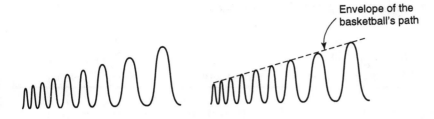

Envelope of the
basketball's path

This is a complex series of movements, that are difficult to describe. One way to simplify these movements is to draw the envelope of the basketball's movement, as shown on the right, above. All we have done here is to connect the points of maximum displacement of the basketball with a line. Although we have lost some information about the ball's movement, we do have a good idea of how high the basketball was being dribbled as the player moved down court.

The envelope of the traveling wave is similar to this. We are dealing here not with a bouncing basketball, but with a complex waveform that moves down the basilar membrane. We can describe this waveform by stopping it at a number of points in time (see Figure 11.27). Or, we can simplify by connecting the peaks of the momentary positions of the traveling wave to create the envelope of the traveling wave (dashed line in Figure 11.27).

Just as in the case of the basketball's movement we lose information here, but in simplifying, we get a clear picture of a very important piece of information - how much the basilar membrane vibrates at each position along its length. This is important because it tells us how vigorously the hair cells vibrate that correspond to each of the positions along the basilar membrane.

<u>The Effect of Masking and Measurement of the Psychophysical Tuning Curve</u> (330)

The nature of the basilar membrane's vibration has been determined by researchers using both physiological and psychophysical evidence. Two psychophysical approaches to determining the nature of basilar membrane vibration are described on pages 330 - 333 of the text. Table 11.1 summarizes the procedures and results for these two approaches.

Table 11.1. Masking and the Psychophysical Tuning Curve

Phenomenon	Number of Masking Tones	What is Measured?	Result and Conclusion
Masking	One high-intensity masking tone is present	The change in threshold across the frequency range caused by the presence of the masking tone.	Result: Masker affects hearing asymmetrically over the frequency range (Figure 11.33). Conclusion: This pattern is similar to the pattern of basilar membrane vibration. (Figure 11.34)
Psychophysical tuning curve	A series of high-intensity masking tones with different frequencies are presented.	The intensity of the masking tone needed to decrease the perception of a single low-intensity test tone to threshold.	Result: The low-intensity test tone is reduced to threshold most easily by masking tones with frequencies near the test tone frequency. Conclusion: The low intensity tone affects a small area of the basilar membrane, thus supporting place theory.

KEY TERMS: CHAPTER 11

Acoustic stimulus. Physical pressure changes in the air that potentially can cause the perception of sound.

Amplitude. In the case of a repeating sound wave, such as the sine wave of a pure tone, amplitude represents the pressure difference between atmospheric pressure and the maximum pressure of the wave.

Apex of the basilar membrane. The end of the basilar membrane farthest from the middle ear.

Area centralis. The horizontal area of high receptor density found in some animals, such as the turtle.

Auditory canal. The canal through which air vibrations travel from the environment to the tympanic membrane.

Auditory masking. A psychophysical technique in which one sound is presented that decreases (masks) a person's ability to hear another sound.

Auditory receiving area. The area of the cortex, located in the temporal lobe, that is the primary receiving area for hearing.

Base of the basilar membrane. The part of the basilar membrane nearest the middle ear.

Basilar membrane. A membrane that stretches the length of the cochlea and controls the vibration of the cochlear partition.

Central pitch processor. A hypothetical central mechanism that analyzes the pattern of a tone's harmonics and selects the fundamental frequency that is most likely to have been part of that pattern.

Characteristic frequency. The frequency at which a neuron in the auditory system has its lowest threshold.

Cilia. Fine hairs that protrude from the inner and outer hair cells of the auditory system. Bending the cilia of the inner hair cells leads to transduction.

Cochlea. The snail-shaped, liquid-filled structure that contains the structures of the inner ear, the most important of which are the basilar membrane, the tectorial membrane, and the hair cells.

Cochlear nucleus. The nucleus where nerve fibers from the cochlea first synapse.

Cochlear partition. A partition in the cochlea, extending almost its full length, that separates the scala tympani and the scala vestibuli.

Cross-modality matching. A subject is presented with a stimulus of one modality and is asked to adjust a stimulus in another modality to match its magnitude.

Decibel (dB). A unit that indicates the presence of a tone relative to a reference pressure: $dB = 20 \log (p/p_0)$ where p is the pressure of the tone and p_0 is the reference pressure.

Direct sound. Sound that is transmitted to the ears directly from a sound source.

Eardrum. Another term for the tympanic membrane, the membrane located at the end of the auditory canal that vibrates in response to sound.

Effect of the missing fundamental. See Periodicity pitch.

Efferent feedback. Signals that travel from higher levels toward the periphery. An example of efferent feedback in the auditory system is a signal that is transmitted from the superior olivary nucleus to the hair cells.

Envelope of the traveling wave. A curve that indicates the maximum displacement at each point along the basilar membrane caused by a traveling wave.

Fourier frequency spectrum. The sine-wave components that make up a periodic waveform. The Fourier spectra of a sound stimulus is usually depicted by a line for each sine-wave frequency, the height of the line indicating the amount of energy at that frequency.

Frequency sweep detector. A neuron in the auditory cortex that fires only when frequencies are smoothly increased or decreased.

Frequency tuning curve. Curve relating the threshold intensity for stimulating an auditory neuron and frequency.

Frequency. In the case of a sound wave that repeats itself like the sine wave of a pure tone, frequency is the number of times per second that the wave repeats itself.

Fundamental frequency. Usually the lowest frequency in the Fourier spectrum of a complex tone. The tone's other components, called harmonics, have frequencies that are multiples of the fundamental frequency.

Hair cells, inner. Auditory receptor cells in the inner ear that are primarily responsible for auditory transduction and the perception of pitch.

Hair cells, outer. Auditory receptor cells in the inner ear that amplify the respond of the inner hair cells (see motile response).

Hair cells. Neurons in the cochlea that contain small hairs, or cilia, that are displaced by vibrations of the basilar membrane. There are two kinds of hair cells: inner and outer

Harmonics. Fourier components of a complex tone with frequencies that are multiples of the fundamental frequency.

Hertz (Hz). The unit for designating the frequency of a tone. One Hertz equals one cycle per second.

Incus. The second of the three ossicles of the middle ear. It transmits vibrations from the malleus to the stapes.

Inferior colliculus. A nucleus in the hearing system along the pathway from the cochlea to the auditory cortex. The inferior colliculus receives inputs from the superior olivary nucleus.

Inner ear. The innermost division of the ear, containing the cochlea and the receptors for hearing.

Inner hair cells. See Hair cells, inner.

Malleus. The first of the ossicles of the middle ear. Receives vibrations from the tympanic membrane and transmits these vibrations to the incus.

Masking. See Auditory masking.

Medial geniculate nucleus. A nucleus in the auditory system along the pathway from the cochlea to the auditory cortex. The medial geniculate nucleus receives inputs from the inferior colliculus.

Middle ear. The small air-filled space between the auditory canal and the cochlea that contains the ossicles.

Middle-ear muscles. Muscles attached to the ossicles in the middle ear. The smallest skeletal muscles in the body, they contract in response to very intense sounds and dampen the vibration of the ossicles.

Motile response. A response to sound of the outer hair cells in which the cells move. The cells tilt and get slightly longer, which amplifies basilar membrane vibration and therefore amplifies the response of the inner hair cells.

Octave. Tones that have frequencies that are binary multiples of each other(x2, x4, etc.). For example, an 800-Hz tone is one octave above a400-Hz tone.

Organ of Corti. The major structure of the cochlear partition, containing the basilar membrane, the tectorial membrane, and the receptors for hearing.

Ossicles. Three small bones in the middle ear that transmit vibrations from the outer to the inner ear.

Outer ear. The pinna and the external auditory meatus.

Outer hair cells. See Hair cells, outer.

Oval window. A small membrane-covered hole in the cochlea that receives vibrations from the stapes.

Periodicity. The repetition of a sound wave's pattern.

Periodicity pitch. The effect in which a complex tone's pitch remains the same even if we eliminate the fundamental frequency. This is also called the effect of the missing fundamental.

Pinna. The part of the ear that is visible on the outside of the head.

Phase locking. Auditory neurons' firing in synchrony with the phase of an auditory stimulus.

Pitch. The quality of sound, ranging from low to high, that is most closely associated with the frequency of a tone.

Place code for frequency. The idea that the frequency of a tone is signaled by the place in the auditory system that is maximally stimulated.

Psychophysical tuning curve. A function that indicates the intensity of masking tones of different frequencies that cause a low-intensity pure tone to become just barely detectable.

Pure tone. A tone with pressure changes that can be described by a single sine wave.

Resonance. A mechanism that enhances the intensity of certain frequencies because of the reflection of sound waves in a closed tube. Resonance occurs in the auditory canal.

Resonance theory. Helmholtz's theory of pitch perception, which proposed that the basilar membrane is made up of a series of transverse fibers, each tuned to resonate to a specific frequency.

Resonant frequency. The frequency that is most strongly enhanced by resonance. The resonance frequency of a closed tube is determined by the length of the tube.

Round window. A small membrane-covered opening at the end of the scala tympani in the cochlea of the ear.

Saturation (nerve firing). The intensity at which a nerve fiber reaches its maximum response. Once the fiber is saturated, further increases in intensity cause no further increase in the fiber's firing rate.

Secondary auditory cortex. Auditory area A2, located next to the primary auditory area (A1).

Sound pressure level (SPL). A designation used to indicate that the reference pressure used for calculating a tone's decibel rating is set at 2×10^{-5} Pascal's, near the threshold in the most sensitive frequency range for hearing.

Sound stimulus. See Acoustic stimulus.

Sound waves. Pressure changes in a medium. Most of the sounds we hear are due to pressure changes in the air.

Sound. The experience of hearing. Sound also refers to the physical stimulus for hearing. To avoid confusion, the term acoustic stimulus or sound stimulus can be used to denote the physical sound stimulus.

Stapes. The last of the three ossicles in the middle ear. It receives vibrations from the incus and transmits these vibrations to the oval window of the inner ear.

Superior olivary nucleus. A nucleus along the auditory pathway from the cochlea to the auditory cortex. The superior olivary nucleus receives inputs from the cochlear nucleus.

Synesthesia. Occurs when stimulation of one modality leads to perceptual experience in another modality, as when hearing sounds results in the perception of colors.

Tectorial membrane. A membrane that stretches the length of the cochlea and is located directly over the hair cells. Vibrations of the cochlear partition cause the tectorial membrane to stimulate the hair cells by rubbing against them.

Timbre. The quality of a tone. Different musical instruments have different timbres, so when we play the same note on different instruments, the notes have the same pitch but sound different.

Tone chroma. Perceptual similarity of tones separated by octaves.

Tone height. The increase in pitch that occurs as frequency is increased.

Timing code of frequency. The sensory code for the frequency of an auditory stimulus in which stimulus frequency is signaled by the timing of nerve impulses in nerve fibers or groups of nerve fibers.

Tonotopic map. The frequency map that is formed on an auditory structure when neurons with the same characteristic frequency are grouped together and neurons with nearby characteristic frequencies are found near each other.

Traveling wave. In the auditory system, vibration of the basilar membrane in which the peak of the vibration travels from the base of the membrane to its apex.

Tuning curve, frequency. See Frequency tuning curve.

Tympanic membrane (eardrum). A membrane at the end of the auditory canal that vibrates in response to vibrations of the air and transmits these vibrations to the ossicles in the middle ear.

Volley principle. Wever's idea that groups of nerve fibers fire in volleys, some fibers firing while others are refractory. In this way, groups of fibers can effect high rates of nerve firing.

White noise. An auditory stimulus that creates an band of frequencies with equal sound pressure at each frequency.

TEST YOURSELF

Indicate the structures in this cross section of the ear. See Figure 11.10 to check your answers.

Divisions of ear

Outer | Middle | Inner

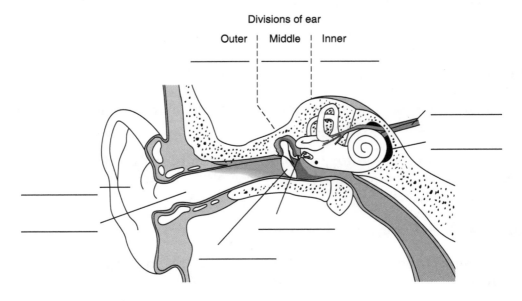

Indicate the structures in this cross section of the organ of Corti. See Figure 11.17 to check your answers.

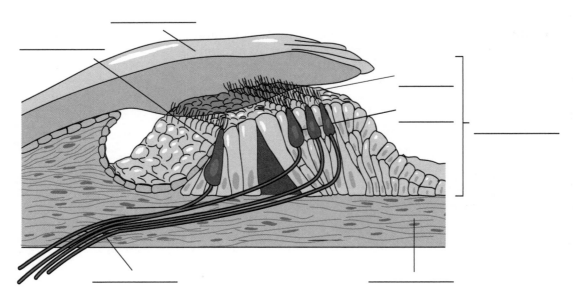

MULTIPLE CHOICE QUESTIONS

11.1 Pure tones (6)
   a) are characterized by a sinusoidal change in pressure
   b) are characterized by pressure vibrations that remain at a constant amplitude
   c) are distortion-free tones
   d) are tones in which the height of the sound wave equals the width of the sound wave

11.2 The decibel is determined by an equation in which _____ is the main term. (8)
   a) loudness
   b) frequency
   c) pressure
   d) time

11.3 If the fundamental frequency of a complex tone is 400 Hz, then the third harmonic will be (11)
   a) 600 Hz
   b) 1,200 Hz
   c) 1,600 Hz
   d) 2,400 Hz

11.4 The auditory canal functions to (17)
   a) protect the structures of the middle ear
   b) amplify some frequencies
   c) connect the middle and inner ear
   d) a and b

11.5 The ossicles are found in the _____ ear. (19)
   a) outer
   b) middle
   c) inner
   d) outer and middle

11.6 The function of the middle ear muscles is to (23)
   a) amplify the sound signal
   b) hold the middle ear bones together
   c) protect the ear against possible damage
   d) help move the ossicles in response to sound

11.7 Most of the fibers in the auditory nerve receive
   signals from the _____ hair cells.(26)
   a) inner
   b) outer

11.8 Who is responsible for the modern version of the place
   theory of hearing? (33, a)
   a) Bekesy
   b) Helmholtz
   c) Young
   d) Wever

11.9 A 4,000 Hz tone will cause a maximal deflection of the
   basilar membrane that is _____ the deflection caused
   by an 8,000 Hz tone.(35)
   a) closer to the base than
   b) farther away from the base than
   c) the same distance from the base as

11.10 The results of masking experiments show that the
   masking tone affects frequencies (37)
   a) on either side of the masking tone equally
   b) greater than the masking tone more strongly
   c) lower than the masking tone more strongly

11.11 Which of the hair cells has a motile response to
   sound? (39)
   a) outer
   b) inner

11.12 The volley principle of auditory function states that (44)
a) pitch is determined by the point of maximal deflection of the basilar membrane
b) excitation occurs every time the basilar membrane vibrates in the upward direction
c) some fibers fire while others are resting
d) the frequency of nerve firing matches the frequency of the sound stimulus

11.13 Most explanations of periodicity pitch focus on (47, 48)
a) the basilar membrane
b) more central structures

11.14 Efferent feedback occurs when (53)
a) signals cross over from one side of the auditory system to another
b) signals in the auditory system travel in separated, parallel pathways
c) signals are sent from higher levels in the auditory system back to the cochlea
d) the middle ear muscles contract in response to high intensity sounds

11.15 In synesthesia, the strongest associations have been reported between (56)
a) color and touch
b) light and sound
c) brightness and pitch
d) color and vowel sounds

CHAPTER 12:

LOUDNESS, SOUND QUALITY, LOCATION, AND THE AUDITORY SCENE

This chapter follows and builds upon the basis established in Chapter 11, by considering the auditory qualities of loudness, quality and location.

CHAPTER ORGANIZATION

1. The nature of loudness and how it depends on frequency.

2. Determinants of the quality of sound. This includes a sound's timbre and also what happens when sound is reflected from surfaces before reaching the listener.

3. How we identify various sound sources in the environment and cause certain sounds to become perceptually organized.

4. How sounds are located in space. This includes both characteristics of stimuli that determine auditory localization and the physiological mechanisms of auditory localization.

5. How sound can be used as information by the visually impaired.

6. How we can study sound from an ecological perspective.

TABLE OF CONTENTS AND KEY TERMS

173

NOTES: CHAPTER 12

The Audibility Curve

The audibility curve, which is a plot of sound pressure level at the threshold for hearing vs. frequency (Figure 12.2) provides information about how loud a stimulus will sound. One thing that the audibility curve tells us is that knowing the sound intensity in decibels tells us nothing about how loud a sound is unless we know the sound's frequency.

Here are some things that the audibility function tells us:

1. All points that are on the audibility function have the same loudness - since they are at threshold, they are all just barely audible. Thus, a 50 Hz tone of 50 decibels and a 1,000 Hz tone of 0 decibels both have the same, near-zero loudness.

2. Tones with any combination of decibels and frequencies that fall above the audibility curve can be heard. Tones with any combination that fall below the curve cannot be heard.

3. All points on a particular equal loudness function (the curves in Figure 12.2 that are above the audibility function) have the same loudness. Since these curves are all above the audibility function, tones represented by these curves are all easy to hear.

4. Consider the dashed horizontal line at 10 dB in Figure 12.2. Tones on the far left of that line will not be audible because they are below the audibility function. When we move to the right, we hit the audibility function at about 400 Hz. This means that a 10 dB, 400- Hz tone will be at threshold - just barely audible. As we continue to move to the right, tones are now above the audibility function and so would be audible. Generally, the higher they are above the audibility function, the louder they will be. However, when the dashed line intersects the audibility curve at about 12,000 Hz, we have again reached threshold, so a 12,000-Hz, 10-dB tone will be just barely audible. Moving further to the right, all 10 dB tones above 12,000 Hz are below the audibility curve and are, therefore, not audible.

The Physiological Basis of Auditory Localization

A number of different kinds of neurons have been discovered that could play a role in auditory localization. Table 12.1 summarizes the ones described in the text:

Table 12.1: Neurons that may be involved in auditory localization.

Type Of Neuron	Properties Of Neuron
Interaural time difference detector (369)	Responds best to specific interaural time differences
Directionally selective neuron (369)	Responds best to sound moving in a particular direction (For example, to the left or the right)
Azimuth sensitive neuron (370)	Responds to sounds in a particular position in space. The tuning of these neurons is, however, broad.
Panoramic neuron (370)	Responds to all sounds no matter where they are. Indicates location by a particular pattern of firing for each direction.
Owl MLD cell (371)	Each neuron responds to a small area of space (more precise tuning than the cat and monkey azimuth sensitive neurons described above).

Acoustic shadow. Shadow created by the head that blocks high-frequency sounds from getting to the opposite side of the head.

Attack. The buildup of sound at the beginning of a tone.

Audibility curve. A curve that indicates the sound pressure level (SPL) at threshold for frequencies across the audible spectrum.

Auditory localization. The perception of the location of a sound source.

Auditory response area. The psychophysically measured area that defines the frequencies and sound pressure levels over which hearing functions. This area extends between the audibility curve and the curve for the threshold of feeling.

Auditory scene analysis. The process by which listeners sort superimposed vibrations into separate sounds

Auditory scene. The sound environment, which includes the locations and qualities of individual sound sources.

Auditory stream segregation. The effect that occurs when a series of tones that differ in pitch are played so that the high- and low-pitched tones alternate so rapidly, that the high and low pitches become perceptually separated into simultaneously occurring independent streams of sound.

Azimuth-sensitive neurons. Neurons in the auditory cortex that respond best to a sound's left-right position in space.

Binaural cells. Neurons in the auditory system that receive inputs from both ears.

Binaural cues. Sound localization cues that involve both ears.

Binocular deprivation. Depriving an animal of vision in both eyes during some portion of their development.

Center frequency. The frequency positioned midway between the lower and upper frequencies in a complex sound stimulus such as noise.

Decay. The decrease in sound at the end of a tone.

Directionally-sensitive neurons. Neurons in auditory cortex that respond to the direction in which a sound stimulus is moving.

Direct sound. Sound that is transmitted to the ears directly from a sound source.

Effect of the missing fundamental. See Periodicity pitch.

Equal loudness curve. A curve that indicates the sound pressure levels that result in a perception of the same loudness at frequencies across the audible spectrum.

Everyday listening. Listening that focuses on events such as an air conditioner blowing or a chair squeaking. (See Musical listening)

Flow pattern. Pattern of visual stimulation that is created as elements in the environment flow past an observer due to observer motion.

Indirect sound. Sound that reaches the ears after being reflected from a surface such as a room's walls.

Interaural differences. Differences in the stimuli reaching the left and right ears, especially the intensity and frequency of the stimuli.

Interaural intensity difference. The greater intensity of a sound at the closer ear when a sound source is positioned closer to one ear than to the other. This effect is most pronounced for high-frequency tones.

Interaural time difference detector. A neuron that fires only when a stimulus is presented first to one ear and then to the other, with a specific delay between the stimulation of the two ears.

Interaural time difference. The effect that, when a sound source is positioned closer to one ear than to the other, the sound reaches the close ear slightly before reaching the far ear.

Large-diameter fiber (L-fiber). According to gate control theory, activity in L-fibers closes the gate control mechanism and therefore decreases the perception of pain. (14)

Localization cues. Information that is used to locate sound sources.

Localization. See Auditory localization.

Loudness. The quality of sound that ranges from soft to loud. For a tone of a particular frequency, loudness usually increases with increasing decibels.

Melodic channeling. See Scale illusion.

Melody schema. A representation of a familiar melody that is stored in a person's memory.

Missing fundamental, effect of. See Periodicity pitch.

Monaural localization cue. Information for sound localization that reaches only one ear.

Musical listening. Listening that focuses on the perceptual qualities of a sound - things such as a sound's pitch or timbre. (See Everyday listening)

Panoramic neuron. A neuron in the auditory system that fires to sounds originating in any direction and which indicates each location by its temporal pattern of firing.

Periodicity pitch. The effect in which a complex tone's pitch remains the same even if we eliminate the fundamental frequency. This is also called the effect of the missing fundamental.

Precedence effect. The effect that occurs when two identical or very similar sounds reach a listener's ears separated by a time interval of less than about 50-100 msec, and the listener hears the sound that reaches his or her ears first.

Reverberation time. The time it takes for a sound produced in an enclosed space to decrease to 1/1000 of its original pressure.

Scale illusion. An illusion that occurs when successive notes of a scale are presented alternately to the left and the right ears. Even though each ear receives notes that jump up and down in frequency, smoothly ascending or descending scales are heard in each ear.

Sone. Unit of loudness. One sone is the loudness of a 1,000-Hz tone at 40 dB.

Sound source. Anything that creates sound stimuli.

TEST YOURSELF

MULTIPLE CHOICE QUESTIONS

12.1 The auditory response area is (3)
   a) the area in space within which we can accurately localize sounds
   b) the area best served by each ear
   c) the region between the audibility curve and the threshold for feeling
   d) the area directly below the audibility curve

12.2 Knowing that a pure tone is 40-dB-SPL enables us to estimate its loudness. (5)
   a) True
   b) False

12.3 If two tones have the same pitch and loudness, but sound different, then they differ in (9)
   a) timbre
   b) tone height
   c) tone chroma
   d) their fundamental frequencies

12.4 A greater proportion of the sound reaching a listener's ears will be direct sound if the listener is (10)
   a) outside
   b) inside

12.5 If you position yourself between two speakers that are playing identical music so you can hear the sound coming from both speakers, and then move a small distance towards one of the speakers, the sound appears to be coming only from the nearer speaker. This occurs because (11)
   a) the sound from the nearer speaker has become louder (because you are closer)
   b) the nearer speaker looks closer
   c) the sound from the near speaker reaches your ears first
   d) indirect sound is suppressed

12.6 Melody schema (14)
   a) refers to the fact that tones that are similar in pitch become perceptually grouped
   b) illustrates the effect of expectation on perception
   c) shows that it is easier to separate two melodies if they are coming from different directions
   d) occurs under conditions that favor melodic channeling

12.7 If high and low tones are alternated slowly, they are heard in a hi-lo-hi-lo pattern. If they are alternated more rapidly, they separate into a high stream and a low stream. This separation into two streams illustrates the law of (14, 15)
   a) proximity
   b) good figure
   c) auditory goodness
   d) good continuation

12.8 Which of the following is not one of the three coordinates that are used to describe auditory localization? (19)
   a) azimuth
   b) elevation
   c) angular
   d) distance

12.9 The localization cue of interaural intensity difference works for (22)
   a) low frequency tones
   b) high frequency tones
   c) both low and high frequency tones

12.10 Which of the following is a monaural cue for sound localization? (23)
   a) interaural intensity difference
   b) interaural time difference
   c) pinnae cues
   d) echo-ranging

12.11 It has been hypothesized that "panoramic" neurons in the cat's cortex play an important role in (25)
a) auditory localization
b) pitch perception
c) intensity discrimination
d) sensing the wide frequency ranges that occur in the environment

12.12 Although it has been shown that bats can use echoes to determine the distance of objects, research indicates that humans cannot make use of this information. (30)
a) True
b) False

12.13 If I describe what I am hearing as "a pitch of about 440 Hz," this would be an example of (32)
a) musical listening
b) everyday listening

12.14 Research shows that the sound of fingernails scratching a blackboard is unpleasant, because of the _____ frequency components of the sound. (36)
a) high
b) low

12.15 If a cat is deprived of binocular vision from birth, so they do not develop binocular neurons, and are then tested on their ability to localize sounds as adults, these cats are _____ normally sighted cats in their ability to localize sounds. (38)
a) equal to
b) worse than
c) more accurate than

CHAPTER 13

PERCEIVING SPEECH

The main problem of speech perception is that although we can measure the complex pattern of pressure changes in the speech stimulus, researchers haven't been able to match up all speech sounds with particular patterns of pressure changes. They have, however, been able to demonstrate some connections between stimulus and sound and have shown how perceptual constancy, which we introduced in Chapter 6, also holds for speech perception. Speech perception also provides examples of multimodal perception (connections between two or more senses) and cognitive effects on perception.

CHAPTER ORGANIZATION

1. The speech stimulus. How the pressure changes associated with the speech stimulus are displayed on a sound spectrogram.

2. Two reasons speech perception is so difficult to explain: (a) the segmentation problem (we hear individual words even though there are no breaks in the speech stimulus); (b) the variability problem (the same sound can be produced in many different ways.

3. How the perception of speech is related to the sound stimulus, describing (a) the search for links between the sound signal and perception of phonemes; (b) conditions under which the stimulus changes but speech perception remains constant, (categorical perception); and (c) how speech perception is influenced by vision (the McGurk effect).

4. How the perception of speech influenced by cognitive factors, emphasizing research that shows how top-down processing facilitates the perception of words and phonemes.

5. The physiological bases of speech perception, including the relation between neural responding and speech perception and brain areas involved in speech perception.

6. We consider the following question: Is there a special mechanism for speech perception, or do we perceive speech using the same mechanisms used to perceive other sounds?

TABLE OF CONTENTS AND KEY TERMS

Constancy and Speech Perception

From Chapter 6 we know that constancy is the situation in which perception remains the same even though the stimulus changes. For example, size perception remains constant even when changes in distance changes the size of the retinal image. Table 13.1 describes three examples of constancy in speech perception.

Table 13.1: Examples of constancy in speech perception

Phenomenon	Description
Coarticulation (386)	A phoneme's sound remains the same even when the phoneme appears in different words or sentences that change the phoneme's acoustic signal.
Categorical perception (390)	Large changes in voice onset time cause no change in perception of a phoneme's sound (perception changes only after the phonetic boundary is crossed).
Speaker variability (386)	Different speakers create speech that varies drastically in accent, tone and rate, yet we still perceive the meaning of what is said. This is constancy of meaning, rather than perception, since the speech sounds change but meaning stays the same. (For coarticulation and categorical perception, the sounds that people hear remain constant).

Cognition and Speech Perception

Speech perception provides a rich source of examples of how cognition affects perception. Table 13.2 lists the examples that appear in the text.

Table 13.2 Examples of how cognition affects speech perception.

Example	Description
Phoneme (382)	The phoneme is defined in terms of its effect on meaning. It is the smallest segment of speech that, if changed, changes the meaning of a word.
Phonemes in context (393)	It is easier to perceive phonemes in a meaningful context (Rubin et. al.)
Phonemic restoration effect (394)	Phonemes are perceived in meaningful sentences, even if the acoustic signal for the phoneme is obscured by a noise like a cough (Warren)
Perceiving degraded sentences (392)	The meaning of a sentence can be perceived, even if many letters are omitted (see Demonstration, page 392).
Segmentation (392)	Even when there are no breaks in the acoustic signal, we still hear individual words. We achieve this based on our knowledge of the word's meaning.

Table 13.2 (continued)

Example	Description
Meaning and word perception (395)	Words are perceived more accurately in meaningful sentences than in non-grammatical strings (Miller and Isard) When parts of words are replaced by electronic noise, they are easier to perceive when in a meaningful sentence and when the beginning of the word is present. (Salassoo and Pisoni)
Indexical characteristics of speaker's voice (396)	Characteristics of a speaker's voice such as intonation, emotional tone, etc. are used to help determine the meaning of what is being said.
Familiarity with speaker's voice (398)	If listener is familiar with a voice from past exposure, he or she can more easily identify a word in a sequence as new or old (Palmeri, et. al.) If listener is familiar with a voice, from prior exposure, it is easier to recognize that voice later (Nygaard et. al.)

Multimodal Nature of Speech Perception

Speech perception can be affected by input from other senses, or can be achieved using information from other senses.

<u>Table 13.3</u> Examples of the multimodal nature of speech perception

Phenomenon	Description
McGurk effect (391)	Perception of lip movements that don't match the acoustic signal can change the perception of what is being said.
Tadoma (401)	People can perceive speech with their fingers and hands, based on tactile information.

Acoustic cues. The sound energy associated with a particular phoneme.

Acoustic signal. The pattern of frequencies and intensities of the sound stimulus.

Aphasia. Difficulties in speaking or understanding speech due to brain damage.

Articulators. Structures involved in speech production, such as the tongue, lips, teeth, jaw, and soft palate.

Audio-visual speech perception. A perception of speech that is affected by both auditory and visual stimulation, as when a person sees a tape of someone saying /ga/ with the sound /ba/ substituted and perceives /da/.

Categorical perception. In speech perception, perceiving one sound at short voice onset times and another sound at longer voice onset times. The listener perceives only two categories across the whole range of voice onset times.

Coarticulation. The overlapping articulation of different phonemes.

Duplex perception. The result when one stimulus causes a person to hear both speech and nonspeech sounds simultaneously.

Formant transitions. In the speech stimulus, the rapid shifts in frequency that precede formants.

Formants. Horizontal bands of energy in the speech spectrogram that are associated with vowels.

Indexical characteristics. Characteristics of the speech stimulus that indicate speaker characteristics such as age, gender and emotional state.

Invariant acoustic cues. In speech perception, aspects of an auditory signal that remain constant even in different contexts.

Manner of articulation. The mechanical means by which consonants are produced and how air is pushed through openings in the vocal tract.

McGurk effect. See Audio-visual speech perception.

Phoneme. The shortest segment of speech that, if changed, would change the meaning of a word.

Phonemic restoration effect. An effect that occurs in speech perception when listeners perceive a phoneme in a word even though the acoustic signal of that phoneme is obscured by another sound.

Phonetic boundary. The voice onset time when perception changes from one speech category to another in a categorical perception experiment.

Place of articulation. The place where the airstream is obstructed during the production of a sound.

Running spectral display. A way of representing the speech stimulus in which a number of short-term spectra are arranged to show how the frequencies in the speech stimulus change as time progresses.

Shadowing. Subjects' repetition aloud of what they hear as they are hearing it.

Short-term spectrum. A plot that indicates the frequencies in a sound stimulus during a short period, usually at the beginning of the stimulus.

Sound spectrogram. A plot showing the pattern of intensities and frequencies of a speech stimulus.

Tadoma. A method of tactile speech perception in which a person identifies speech sounds by feeling the vibrations of a speaker's vocal cords.

Voice onset time. In speech production, the time delay between the beginning of a sound and the beginning of the vibration of the vocal chords.

Wernicke's aphasia. An inability to comprehend words or arrange sounds into coherent speech.

MULTIPLE CHOICE QUESTIONS

13.1 Just as powerful computers can now beat people at chess, computers can also rival humans' ability to perceive speech (1)
a) True
b) False

13.2 The frequencies characteristic of different vowels are determined by (6)
a) of the shape of the vocal tract
b) the length of the bursts of energy for different vowels
c) the frequency of vibration of the vocal cords
d) the speed at which a speaker speaks

13.3 A sound spectrogram (8)
a) is a listing of all of the phonemes that make up a word
b) is a plot of sound intensity vs. frequency
c) is a plot of frequency vs. time
d) indicates the SPL in decibels which can just barely be heard at each frequency

13.4 By looking at the spectrogram for a sentence, we can identify where one word ends and the other begins (11)
a) True
b) False

13.5 The variability problem in speech perception refers to the fact that (12)
a) two phonemes may sometimes share the same phonetic features
b) if we look at the spectrograms of many people's speech we see that there are usually no spaces between words
c) a specific phoneme is not always associated with the same acoustic cue
d) two people can hear the same speech sounds, but interpret them differently

13.6 Researchers have been able to identify invariant
     acoustic cues for all of the speech sounds in English.
     (20)
     a) True
     b) False

13.7 A listener can discriminate between two sounds in a
     categorical perception only if they are on _____ of
     the phonetic boundary. (24)
     a) the same side
     b) different sides

13.8 Which of the following provides an example of
     perceptual constancy in speech perception? (14, 25)
     a) coarticulation
     b) categorical perception
     c) audio-visual speech perception
     d) a and b

13.9 The auditory system fills in missing sounds based on
     the context surrounding the sound. This is a
     description of (33)
     a) verbal summation
     b) the verbal transformation effect
     c) the phonemic restoration effect
     d) syntactical prediction

13.10 In Salassoo and Pisoni's experiment in which they had
      subjects write down what they heard for words that
      were presented in meaningful sentences, in strange
      sentences, and alone, they found that (37)
      a) less of the word needs to be present if the
         beginning of the word is included
      b) accuracy of identification depended on the
         percentage of the word present, not what part of
         the word is present
      c) less of the word needs to be present if the end of
         the word is included

13.11 Information about things such as a speaker's age, gender, and emotional state are contained in (38)
a) phonemic characteristics
b) indexical characteristics
c) invariant cues
d) the speech signal's formants

13.12 Speech is lateralized on the _____ side of the brain for most people (44)
a) left
b) right

13.13 The phenomenon of duplex perception has been used to argue that speech is (50)
a) multimodal
b) uniquely human
c) variable
d) special

13.14 PET studies show that pitch stimuli activate areas in the _____ hemisphere and speech stimuli activate areas in the _____ hemisphere. (48)
a) left; left
b) right; right
c) left; right
d) right; left

13.15 The multimodal nature of speech perception is supported by which of the following phenomena? (26, 27, 53)
a) Tadoma
b) categorical perception
c) the McGurk effect
d) a and c

CHAPTER 14

THE CUTANEOUS SENSES

The chapter on cutaneous senses is a good example of how senses that cause very different perceptions can operate according to similar principles. From your knowledge of visual perception, you are already familiar with most of the principles that operate for cutaneous perception. This chapter shows how these principles apply to the cutaneous senses. The section on pain perception also provides especially good examples of how cognition can affect perception.

CHAPTER ORGANIZATION

1. The anatomy of the somatosensory system, including the receptors and central pathways.

2. How evidence from psychophysical and physiological research support the idea that there are four channels for tactile perception that involve four different types of mechanoreceptors.

3. How some neurons are specialized to respond to temperature.

4. How tactile stimuli are processed as they travel through the cutaneous system. This includes a description of how the magnification factor applies to touch (so more cortical space is devoted to structures which are used more and have higher tactile acuity), and the properties of neurons specialized to respond to specific types of stimuli.

5. How tactile perception is affected by active exploration with the fingers and hands (active touch).

6. How pain perception is affected by (a) input from the receptors (bottom-up processing) and (b) knowledge, expectations, and culture (top-down processing)

TABLE OF CONTENTS AND KEY TERMS

Neural Processing Of Tactile Stimuli (416)
   Measuring Tactile Acuity: The Two-Point Threshold
      • **two-point threshold**
   Receptive Fields And Tactile Acuity
   Maps Of The Body On The Cortex: The Magnification Factor
      • **magnification factor**
      • **homunculus**
   Changing The Maps On The Brain: Plasticity Of The Somatosensory
      Cortex
      • **neural plasticity**
   Neurons That Respond To Specialized Stimuli

Active Touch (422)
      • **active touch**
   Using Active Touch To Identify Objects
   Haptic Perception: Tactile Perception Of Three-Dimensional Objects
      • **haptic perception**
      • **exploratory procedures (EPs)**

Pain Perception: Neural Firing And Cognitive Influences (426)
   Neural Responding And Pain Perception
      • **nociceptors**
   Culture, Experience, And Pain Perception
      • **placebo**
   Gate Control Theory
      • **gate control theory**
      • **substantia gelatanosa**
      • **transmission cells**
      • **small diameter fibers**
      • **large diameter fibers**
      • **stimulation produced analgesia**
      • **acupuncture**
      • **analgesia**
      • **active**
   Endorphins
      • **endorphins**
      • **naloxone**
      • **stress-induced analgesia**

NOTES: CHAPTER 14

Almost every principle that holds for the visual system also holds for the cutaneous system. The similarities described in the chapter are summarized in Table 14.1.

Table 14.1 Parallels between the cutaneous and visual systems

Phenomenon	Cutaneous	Visual
Multiple receptor types	Mechanoreceptors and thermoreceptors that are sensitive to specific types of cutaneous stimuli. (407)	Rod and cone receptors that are sensitive to different parts of the spectrum
Receptor properties affect perception	Pacinian corpuscle ending causes the neuron to respond just at onset and offset of the stimuli. (412)	Rod and cone visual pigments determine spectral sensitivity. Pigment regeneration determines dark adaptation.
Magnification factor	Areas with high acuity (small two-point threshold) have magnified space on the cortex. See Figure 14.18. (418)	Foveal cones have magnified space on the cortex .

Table 14.1 (continued)

Phenomenon	Cutaneous	Visual
Receptive fields/specialized neurons	Center-surround receptive fields of thalamic cells. Orientation selective cells in the cortex Directionally selective cells in the cortex. (420)	Center-surround receptive fields of retinal and LGN cells Orientation selective neurons in striate cortex Directionally selective neurons in striate cortex
Parallel pathways	Spinothalamic pathway (small fibers/temperature and pain) and lemniscal pathway (large fibers/touch) (409)	Ventral (what) and dorsal (where or how) pathways.
Columnar organization	Location columns in somatosensory cortex (419)	Location columns in striate cortex
Attention and neural responding	Attention affects firing in S1 and S2 neurons. (421)	Attention affects firing in extrastriate neurons.

Pain Perception

The section on pain perception at the end of the chapter illustrates (a) specialized receptors (nociceptors); (b) parallel pathways (pain is controlled by a number of different kinds of inputs; and (c) how a neural circuit can operate to combine the different inputs that contribute to pain perception (gate control theory); and (d) how factors in addition to stimulation of the receptors influences pain perception. Table 14.2 summarizes a number of the factors that influence pain perception.

Table 14.2: Factors that influence pain perception

Influence	Description
Nociceptors (426)	Stimulation of nociceptors excites small fibers, which results in pain perception.
Cortical neurons in area 7b (426)	Neural firing and behavior go together when the skin is heated (Dong et. al.)
Culture (427)	Examples: The hook swinging ceremony (page 427); Nepalese subjects (page 431)
Expectations (428)	Less pain in hospital when surgical patients know what to expect.
Background/training (432)	Female athletes report less pain than non-athletes

Table 14.2 (continued)

Influence	Description
Emotional state (428)	Morphine causes more pain relief for pain caused by anxiety. Soldiers with battlefield casualties experience less pain than civilian surgical subjects (Beecher)
Stress-induced analgesia (430)	Sensitivity to pain decreases in stressful situations.
Endorphins (430)	Naturally occurring chemicals in the brain that have analgesic effects.
Stimulation produced analgesia (430)	Stimulation of sites in the brain causes analgesia. Note that this works best when endorphin sites are stimulated.
Placebo (430)	Thirty-five percent of patients with pathological pain get relief from a placebo (sugar pill).

KEY TERMS: CHAPTER 14

Active touch. Touch in which the observer plays an active role in touching and exploring an object, usually with his or her hands.

Acupuncture. A procedure in which fine needles are inserted into the skin at specific points. Twirling these needles or passing electrical current through them can cause analgesia.

Analgesia. The elimination of pain without loss of consciousness.

Cold fiber. A nerve fiber that responds to decreases in temperature or to steady low temperatures.

Cutaneous sensations. Sensations based on the stimulation of receptors in the skin.

Dorsal root. The pathway through which fibers from the skin enter the spinal cord.

Efferent fibers. Fibers carrying signals from the brain toward the periphery.

Endorphins. Chemicals that are naturally produced in the brain and that cause analgesia.

Epidermis. The outer layers of the skin, including a layer of dead skin cells.

Exploratory procedures (EPs). People's movements of their hands and fingers while they are identifying three-dimensional objects by touch.

Gate control theory. Melzak and Wall's idea that our perception of pain is controlled by a neural circuit that takes into account the relative amount of activity in large (L) fibers and small (S) fibers.

Haptic perception. The perception of three-dimensional objects by touch.

Homunculus. "Little man," a term referring to the map of the body in the somatosensory cortex.

Kinesthesis. The sense that enables us to feel the motions and positions of the limbs and body.

Large-diameter fiber (L-fiber). According to gate control theory, activity in L-fibers closes the gate control mechanism and therefore decreases the perception of pain.

Magnification factor. The apportioning of proportionally more space on the cortex to the representation of specific areas of sensory receptors. For example, a small area on the retina in or near the fovea receives more space on the cortex than the same area of peripheral retina. Similarly, the fingertips receive more space on the somatosensory cortex than the forearm or leg. (3, 14)

Mechanoreceptor fibers. Fibers that respond to mechanical displacements of the skin. There are two types of mechanoreceptive fibers, rapidly adapting fibers (the two main kinds being RA1 and PC), and slowly adapting fibers (the two main kinds being SAI and SAII).

Medial lemniscal pathway. A pathway in the spinal cord that transmits signals from the skin toward the thalamus.

Meissner corpuscle. A receptor in the skin, associated with RA I mechanoreceptors, that responds best to taps on the skin.

Merkel receptors. Receptors in the skin, associated with SA I mechanoreceptors, that respond best to light pressure and are sensitive to details.

Microneurography. A procedure for recording the activity of single neurons in the skin of awake humans.

Naloxone. A substance that inhibits the activity of opiates. It is hypothesized that naloxone also inhibits the activity of endorphins.

Neural plasticity. The fact that the anatomy and functionality of the nervous system can change in response to experience. Examples are how early visual experience can change the proportion of binocular neurons in the visual cortex, and how tactile experience can change the sizes of areas in the cortex that represent different parts of the body.

Nociceptor. A fiber that responds to stimuli that are damaging to the skin.

Pacinian corpuscle. A receptor with a distinctive elliptical shape associated with RA II mechanoreceptors. It transmits pressure to the nerve fiber inside it only at the beginning or end of a pressure stimulus.

Phantom limb. A person's continued perception of a limb, such as an arm or a leg, even though that limb has been amputated.

Placebo. A substance that a person believes will relieve symptoms such as pain but that contains no chemicals that actually act on these symptoms.

Proprioception. The sensing of the position of the limbs.

Rapidly adapting (RA) fiber. A mechanoreceptive fiber that adapts rapidly to continuous stimulation of the skin. Rapidly adapting fibers are associated with Meissner corpuscle and Pacinian corpuscle receptors.

Ruffini cylinder. A receptor structure in the skin associated with slowly adapting fibers, large receptive fields, and the perception of "buzzing," stretching of the skin, and limb movements.

Secondary somatosensory cortex (S II). The area in the parietal lobe next to the primary somatosensory area (S I) that processes neural signals related to touch, temperature, and pain.

Slowly adapting (SA) fiber. A mechanoreceptive fiber in the skin that adapts slowly to continuous stimulation of the skin. Slowly adapting fibers are associated with Merkel receptors and Ruffini cylinders.

Small-diameter fiber (S-fiber). According to gate control theory, activity in S-fibers opens the gate control mechanism and therefore increases the perception of pain.

Somatosensory receiving area (S1). An area in the parietal lobe of the cortex that receives inputs from the skin and the viscera that are associated with somatic senses such as touch, temperature, and pain. (See Secondary somatosensory receiving area)

Somatosensory system. The system that includes the cutaneous senses (senses involving the skin), proprioception (the sense of position of the limbs), and kinesthesis (sense of movement of the limbs).

Spatial event plots. Plots showing the pattern of response generated by a neuron to a touch stimulus.

Spinothalamic pathway. One of the nerve pathways in the spinal cord that conducts nerve impulses from the skin to the somatosensory area of the thalamus.

Stimulation-produced analgesia (SPA). Brain stimulation that eliminates or strongly decreases the perception of pain.

Stress-induced analgesia. Analgesia that occurs when an organism experiences a stressful situation.

Substantia gelatinosa. A nucleus in the spinal cord that, according to gate control theory, receives inputs from S-fibers and L-fibers and sends inhibition to the T-cell.

Thermoreceptor. Receptors in the skin that responds to specific temperatures or changes in temperature.

Transmission cell (T-cell). According to gate control theory, the cell that receives input from the L- and S-fibers. Activity in the T-cell determines the perception of pain.

Two-point threshold. The smallest separation between two points on the skin that is perceived as two points; a measure of acuity on the skin.

Ventral posterior nucleus. A nucleus in the thalamus that receives inputs from the somatosensory system, primarily from the spinothalamic and lemniscal pathways.

Warm fiber. A nerve fiber that responds to increases in temperature or to steady high temperatures.

TEST YOURSELF

Fill in the identities of the structures indicated in the cross-section of the skin below. See Figure 14.3 to check your answer.

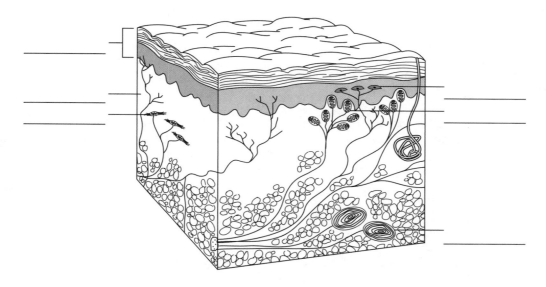

MULTIPLE CHOICE QUESTIONS

14.1 Expert braille readers can read _____ the average visual reader. (1)
   a) faster than
   b) as fast as
   c) about a third as fast as
   d) about a tenth as fast as

14.2 The somatosensory receiving area is in the _____ lobe. (6)
   a) frontal
   b) temporal
   c) parietal
   d) occipital

14.3 The perception associated with the PC channel is (7, 8)
a) pressure
b) tickle
c) vibration
d) pain

14.4 The _____ is a layered onion like receptor located deep in the skin. (5)
a) Meissner corpuscle
b) Merkel receptor
c) Ruffini cylinder
d) Pacinian corpuscle

14.5 Experiments which compared psychophysical and physiological responses to raised letters indicate that _____ fibers are probably important for detailed perception. (11)
a) SAI
b) RAI
c) PC
d) SAII

14.6 Which fibers will fire in response to running the fingers over a textured surface? (13)
a) SA 1 and RA 1
b) RA 1
c) PC
d) all of the above

14.7 In general, smaller receptive fields are associated with (16)
a) smaller two-point thresholds
b) larger two-point thresholds

14.8 Homunculus means (19)
a) many maps
b) heavy touch
c) little man
d) strange shape

14.9 In Hsiao's experiment in which he rolled raised letters over a monkey's finger and recorded from neurons in the somatosensory cortex, he found that (24)
   a) the response was bigger when the monkeys focused their attention on a visual stimulus
   b) the response was bigger when the monkeys focused their attention on the tactile stimulus
   c) there was no difference in the response in the visual and tactile attention conditions, because the experimenter was controlling the stimulus, not the monkey

14.10 Which of the following does not occur in both the visual system and the cutaneous system? (19, 22, 24)
   a) center-surround receptive fields
   b) attention affects neural responding
   c) magnification factor in the cortex
   d) none of the above (they all occur in both the visual and cutaneous systems)

14.11 Passive touch can provide information equal to active touch if the stimulus is (28)
   a) moving
   b) simple
   c) pressed onto the skin
   d) none of the above. Passive touch cannot provide information equal to active touch

14.12 Which of the following is difficult to explain in terms of gate control theory? (34, 36)
   a) the placebo effect
   b) acupuncture
   c) the fact that wounded soldiers request less painkiller than civilians who are having similar operations
   d) none of the above (all of the above can be explained by gate control theory)

14.13 The perception of pain can be influenced by (35, 37, 38)
   a) stress
   b) stimulation of areas away from the pain site
   c) chemicals in the brain
   d) all of the above

14.14 Based on his research on how well blind people can identify raised line drawings, Kennedy has concluded that (45)
   a) people who are blind from birth are unable to identify raised line drawings
   b) both blind people and sighted people wearing blindfolds make use of the somatosensory area of the brain to identify raised line drawings
   c) there may be an amodal region of the brain that interprets inputs from vision and touch in the same way.
   d) there is little difference between the performance of early-blind and late-blind individuals

CHAPTER 15

THE CHEMICAL SENSES

Olfaction and taste are similar in that they both involve the detection of molecules. They are also similar in that we know less about them than the other senses, especially with regard to the nature of the sensory code. This is why, as you read this chapter, you may notice that the answer to the question "what is the code for taste/smell?" is not as clear as for the other senses.

CHAPTER ORGANIZATION

1. Capabilities of human olfaction and the functions of olfaction.

2. The structure of the olfactory system, and how the receptors and other structures respond to odorant molecules.

3. The neural code for odor. This involves a discussion of the response generated by various odorants at different levels of the olfactory system.

4. How taste and smell interact to create flavor.

5. Some of the factors influencing food preference.

6. The structure of the taste system.

7. The basic taste qualities, including a discussion of individual differences in people's sensitivity to them.

8. The neural code for taste quality.

TABLE OF CONTENTS AND KEY TERMS

NOTES: CHAPTER 15

Structure of the olfactory system

The structure of the olfactory system can be confusing, especially since a number of the structures have very similar names.

Table 15.1 Olfactory mucosa structures (443)

Note: The smallest structure is listed first in this table and 15.2.

Structure	Description	Types
Olfactory receptor proteins	Receptor sites located on the cilia of olfactory receptor neurons. (Figures 15.3d, e, f)	About 1,000 types. Each type responds to a small group of odorants.
Olfactory receptor neurons	Individual neurons in the olfactory bulb (Figure 15.3c)	About 1,000 types. Each type has similar olfactory receptor proteins and so responds to a small group of odorants.

Note that there is also a protein called the olfactory binding protein. It floats in the olfactory mucosa ready to pick up odorants and transport them to the receptors. Don't confuse these "transportation" molecules with the similar sounding olfactory receptor neurons or olfactory receptor proteins.

Table 15.2 Olfactory bulb structures (446)

Structure	Description	Types
Glomeruli	Structures that receive inputs predominately from one particular type of receptor neuron. Glomeruli are, therefore, information collection centers for specific types of odorants.	About 1,000 glomeruli, each one of which receives inputs from similar receptor neurons.
Mitral and tufted cells	Neurons in the glomeruli that transmit signals from the glomeruli toward the olfactory cortex.	Mitral and tufted cells are associated with a specific glomerulus.

Olfactory coding

The code for olfactory quality is a combination of specificity and distributed coding. It is specific in that individual receptor neurons respond to specific groups of odorants (with similar odotopes). It is distributed since groups of odorants are involved. Also a particular odorant causes activity over an area of the olfactory mucosa or olfactory bulb, that also responds to other odorants as well.

Table 15.3 Coding in the olfactory mucosa

Structure/Area	Description of responding
Individual receptor neurons (448)	Each responds to a number of odorants, but these odorants are usually similar to each other (they have similar odotopes).
Surface of the mucosa (448)	Similar odorants cause responding in specific areas of the mucosa (regional sensitivity effect). This means that receptors that respond to similar chemicals are grouped together in the mucosa.

Table 15.4 Coding in the olfactory bulb and cortex

Structure/Area	Description of responding
Olfactory glomeruli (449)	Neurons in a glomerulus respond to a number of stimuli, but they usually have similar odotopes.
Areas in olfactory bulb (449)	Different chemicals activate glomeruli that are located in different areas in the olfactory bulb, and glomeruli that respond to similar chemicals are grouped together. This is odotopic mapping.
Orbitofrontal cortex (450)	Single neurons respond to small numbers of odorants (but our information on cortical responding to olfactory stimuli is scanty).

Table 15.5 Peripheral taste system structures

Note: Smaller structures are listed first

Structure	Description
Taste receptors (Figure 15.14e)	Receptors for bitter, sweet, sour, and salt are located on a taste cell.
Taste cell (Figure 15.14c, d)	A number of taste cells are grouped together to form a taste bud. The tips of the taste cells protrude into the taste pore so receptors (located on the tips of the taste cells) can be stimulated.
Taste bud (Figures 15.14 b, c)	Made up of a number of taste cells
Papilla (Figures 15.14 a, b)	Structures on the tongue that contain a number of taste buds.

Table 15.6 Coding the taste system

Evidence for distributed coding:

Structure	Responding
Chorda tympani nerve in the rat (Erickson) (459)	A particular taste stimulus results in a specific pattern of responding across a group of neurons.

Table 15.6 (Continued)

Evidence for specificity coding:

Structure	Responding
Monkey chorda tympani nerve (Sato et. al.) (459)	Four different types of fibers, each type responds best to chemicals representing one of the basic tastes.
Monkey NST neurons in medulla (Jacobs, et. al.) (461)	Sodium deprivation causes a decrease in responding of sodium-active neurons.
Rat NST neurons (Scott and Giza) (461)	Ameloride (blocks sodium channels) decreases response of salt-best fibers.
Human tongue (McCutchen) (461)	Ameloride eliminates perception of salt taste

Alliesthesia. "Changed sensation. " The change in reaction to a stimulus, which may be positive when we first experience it but, after repeated presentations, becomes more negative.

Anosmia. Loss of the ability to smell due to injury or infection.

Chemesthesis. The sense responsible for detecting chemical substances that are irritating or which have a tactile component. Also called the common chemical sense.

Chorda tympani nerve. A nerve that transmits signals from receptors on the front and sides of the tongue.

Common chemical sense. See chemesthesis.

Conditioned flavor aversion. Avoidance of a flavor after it has been paired with sickness.

Electro-olfactogram. An electrical response recorded from the pooled activity of thousands of receptors in the olfactory mucosa.

Flavor. The perception that occurs from the combination of taste and olfaction.

Frontal operculum cortex. An area in the frontal lobe of the cortex that receives signals from the taste system.

Gas chromatograph. A device that accurately measures the concentration of the vapor given off by a chemical stimulus.

Glomeruli. A structure in the olfactory bulb that receives inputs from the receptors. Contains mitral cells and tufted cells that send projections to olfactory areas of the cortex.

Glossopharyngeal nerve. A nerve that transmits signals from receptors located at the back of the tongue.

Insula. An area in the frontal lobe of the cortex that receives signals from the taste system.

Macrosmatic. Having a keen sense of smell that is important to an animal's survival.

Menstrual synchrony. The effect that women who live together often have menstrual periods that begin at approximately the same time.

Microsmatic. Having a weak sense of smell that is not crucial to an animal's survival.

Nasal pharynx. A passageway that connects the mouth cavity and the nasal cavity.

Neurogenesis. The cycle of birth, development, and death of a neuron. This process occurs for the receptors for olfaction and taste.

Nontasters. People who cannot taste the compound phenylthiocarbamide (PTC).

Nucleus of the solitary tract (NST). The nucleus in the brainstem that receives signals from the tongue, the mouth, and the larynx transmitted by the chorda tympani, glossopharyngeal, and vagus nerves.

Odotope. A group of odorants that share a specific chemical feature that determines neural firing.

Odotopic mapping. The way different odors cause activity in different areas of the olfactory bulb.

Olfactometer. A device that presents olfactory stimuli with great precision.

Olfactory binding proteins. Proteins contained in the olfactory mucosa that are secreted into the nasal cavity, bind to olfactory stimuli and transport them to active sites on the olfactory receptors.

Olfactory bulb. The structure that receives signals directly from the olfactory receptors.

Olfactory cortex. A small area under the temporal lobe of the cortex that receives signals that originate in the olfactory receptors.

Olfactory mucosa. The region inside the nose that contains the receptors for the sense of smell.

Olfactory receptor neurons. Neurons in the olfactory mucosa that contain the olfactory receptor proteins that respond to odor stimuli.

Olfactory receptor proteins. Active sites for olfaction on the olfactory cilia of the olfactory receptor neurons.

Orbitofrontal cortex. An area in the frontal lobe, near the eyes, that receives signals originating in the olfactory receptors.

Papillae. Ridges and valleys on the tongue, some of which contain taste buds. There are four types of papillae: filiform, fungiform, foliate, and circumvallate.

Regional sensitivity effect. In the olfactory system, the fact that different areas on the mucosa are sensitive to some odorants and are not as sensitive to others.

Specific hunger. A genetically programmed taste preference that helps organisms seek out food that meets specific nutritional needs.

Taste blind. A person who is taste-blind cannot taste phenylthiocarbamide (PTC) and also tends to be less sensitive to certain other tastes than someone who is not taste-blind.

Taste bud. A structure located within papillae on the tongue that contains the taste cells.

Taste cells. Cells located in taste buds that cause the transduction of chemical to electrical energy when chemicals contact receptor sites or channels located at the tips of these cells.

Taste pore. An opening in the taste bud through which the tips of taste cells protrude. When chemicals enter a taste pore, they stimulate the taste cells and result in transduction.

Tasters. People who can taste the compound phenylthiocarbamide (PTC).

Vagus nerve. A nerve that conducts signals from taste receptors in the mouth and larynx.

Video microscopy. A technique that has been used to take pictures of papillae and taste buds on the tongue.

TEST YOURSELF

Fill in the identities of the structures indicated in these pictures of the olfactory system. See Figure 15.3 to check your answer.

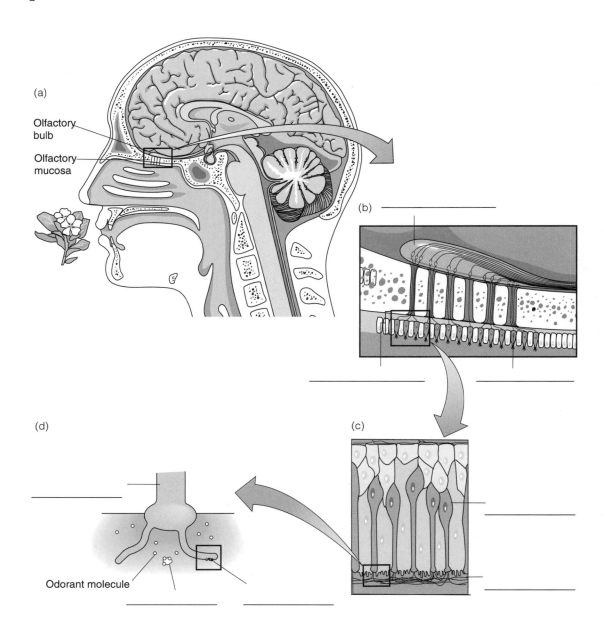

(a)

Olfactory bulb

Olfactory mucosa

(b)

(d)

(c)

Odorant molecule

Fill in the identities of the structures indicated in this diagram of the olfactory mucosa and olfactory bulb. See Figure 15.4 to check your answer.

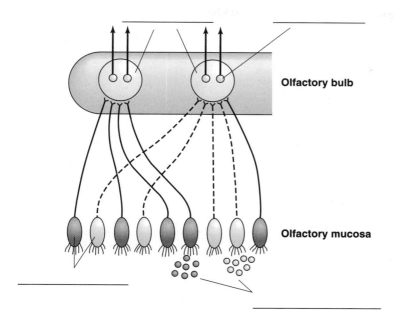

MULTIPLE-CHOICE QUESTIONS

15.1 A property of the taste and smell systems, called neurogenesis is (1)
   a) renewal of the receptors
   b) gatekeeping to keep out harmful substances
   c) molecule detection
   d) genetic determination of molecular sensitivities

15.2 The dog has a greater sensitivity to olfactory stimuli than humans because of the (3)
   a) greater sensitivity of the dog's receptors
   b) orientation of the dog's receptors
   c) greater number of olfactory receptors in the dog
   d) location of the dog's receptors

15.3   With training it is possible for subjects to
        correctly identify the smells of familiar substances
        such as coffee and bananas on almost 100 percent of
        the trials. (5)
        a) True   b) False

15.4   There are about _____ different types of olfactory
        receptor proteins. (10)
        a) 10   c) 1,000
        b) 100   d) 1,000,000

15.5   Each glomerulus in the olfactory system (12)
        a) collects information from a number of different
           types of receptor neurons
        b) receives information predominately from one type
           of receptor neuron
        c) collects information from one place on the
           olfactory mucosa
        d) transmits signals to the olfactory bulb

15.6   Investigations of the olfactory mucosa indicate that
        most areas of the mucosa are equally sensitive to all
        chemicals. (17)
        a) True   b) False

15.7   Odotopic mapping occurs (20)
        a) at the level of the receptor neurons
        b) on the surface of the olfactory mucosa
        c) in the olfactory bulb
        d) in the olfactory cortex

15.8   The perception of flavor is most closely associated
        with (22)
        a) odor stimuli from food
        b) the retronasal route
        c) open nostrils
        d) all of the above are associated with the
           perception of flavor

15.9   Conditioned flavor aversion (25)
        a) occurs when animals avoid flavors that have made
           them sick
        b) occurs when animals avoid food that other animals
           reject
        c) has been demonstrated in animals, but not in
           humans
        d) a and c

15.10 Which of the following structures in the taste system is the <u>smallest</u>? (28)
a) papillae
b) taste buds
c) taste cell
d) taste receptor

15.11 Research using substances such as PTC and PROP has suggested that when two people have different reactions to food (for example, one describes the taste as bitter, the other as neutral) the cause may be (32, 33)
a) differences in the number of taste receptors
b) different past experience with taste substances
c) inborn taste preferences
d) differences in the saliva

15.12 There is no evidence for distributed coding in the taste system (34)
a) True
b) False

15.13 Taking all of the evidence together, most researchers have concluded that taste coding is best described by distributed code. (37)
a) True
b) False

15.14 Just as there is chemical inhibition at synapses, chemical stimuli in the taste system can cause inhibition, so one taste stimulus can inhibit the response caused by another taste stimulus. (39)
a) True
b) False

15.15 The common chemical sense (40)
a) is the ability to sense the basic tastes
b) is the ability to sense familiar substances
c) is the sense that is responsible for detecting irritating chemicals
d) refers to the primitive taste systems in lower animals

CHAPTER 16

PERCEPTUAL DEVELOPMENT

The story of perceptual development is the story of researchers' ability to devise ways to measure the perception of newborns and young infants. Two procedures, preferential looking and habituation, described on pages 470-473 of your text are the ones that are used in most of the experiments described in this chapter. Be sure you understand the basic principles behind these procedures.

CHAPTER ORGANIZATION

1. How infant perception is measured. The focus is on preferential looking and habituation.

2. The perceptual capacities of newborns and how these capacities improve with age, for (1) vision; (2) hearing, and (3) taste and olfaction.

3. How experience affects perceptual development. We describe (1) The physiological and behavioral effects of selective rearing; and (2) how myopia develops in humans.

TABLE OF CONTENTS AND KEY TERMS

NOTES: CHAPTER 16

Developmental Sequences

There are a number of situations in this chapter in which a series of related experiments are described. These related experiments are often done to define the age at which a particular perceptual ability emerges. The Tables below summarize a few of these experiments.

Table 16.1 Sequence of experiments studying face perception in newborns

Condition	Result
Mothers vs. strangers (live) (Bushnell, et. al., 1989)	Mothers preferred
Mothers vs. strangers (video) Walton, et. al., 1992)	Mothers preferred
Mothers vs. strangers (wearing scarf) (Pascalis, et. al., 1995)	No preference

Table 16.2 Two ways to separate figure and ground

Dimension	Experiment
Lightness similarity	Perceptual organization can occur based on lightness similarity in 3-month-old infants. (Quinn et. al., 1993)
Movement	Figure and ground can be separated based on stimulus movement, in 5-month-old infants (Crater and Yonas, 1990)

Table 16.3 Development of the ability to infer that an object exists behind an occluder.

Age	Result
Newborn (479)	Doesn't perceive moving rod as extending behind an occluder. (Slater, et. al., 1990)
2 months (480)	Does perceive rod moving back and forth as extending behind an occluder. (Doesn't perceive this if the rod is stationary). (Johnson and Aslin, 1995)
4 months (479)	Same result as for 2 months (Kellman and Spelke, 1983).

KEY TERMS: CHAPTER 16

Amblyopia. A large reduction in the acuity in one eye.

Amodal representation. An internal description of a stimulus that holds across more than one modality.

Astigmatism. A condition in which vision is blurred in some orientations because of a misshapen cornea.

Binocular fixation. Simultaneously directing the foveas of both eyes at an object.

Dishabituation. An increase in looking time that occurs when a stimulus is changed. This response is used in testing infants to see if they can differentiate two stimuli.

Emmetropia. The condition in which the eye brings the images of objects into accurate focus on the retina.

Emmetropic vision. See emmetropia.

Emmetropization. The developmental process by which emmetropic vision is achieved.

Equivalence classification. In speech perception, the ability to classify vowel sounds as belonging to the same class, even if the speakers are different.

Evoked potential. See Visual evoked potential.

Habituation. The result when the same stimulus is presented repeatedly. For example, infants look at a stimulus less and less on each succeeding trial.

Intermodal matching. Ability to match shapes presented in two different modalities.

Meridional amblyopia. A condition in which a person has an astigmatism that cannot be optically corrected.

Minimum audible angle. The smallest angle between two sound sources that results in the perception of two separate sounds.

Myopia (nearsightedness). The inability to see distant objects clearly because parallel rays of light are brought to a focus in front of the retina.

Preferential looking (PL) technique. A technique used to measure perception in infants. Two stimuli are presented, and the infant's looking behavior is monitored for the amount of time the infant spends viewing each stimulus.

Selective rearing. A technique in which animals are reared in special environments, usually during their sensitive period.

Stereoacuity. The ability to resolve small differences in disparity.

Visual evoked potential (VEP). An electrical response to visual stimulation recorded by the placement of disk electrodes on the back of the head. This potential reflects the activity of a large population of neurons in the visual cortex.

Visual feedback model. Explanation for the development of emmetropia which states that the growth of the eyeball that occurs during this development is controlled by errors in the focusing of light on the retina. Thus, if there is an error in focusing, the eye grows to eliminate this error.

MULTIPLE CHOICE QUESTIONS

16.1   In the habituation procedure the experimenter measures (3)
a) how long it takes for an infant to stop looking at an object
b) the amount of time that an infant looks at each of two simultaneously presented objects
c) the change in looking time that occurs after one stimulus is replaced by another stimulus
d) the number of trials that it takes for an infant's looking time to decrease to half of the looking time measured at the beginning of the experiment

16.2   Visual acuity is low at birth because the newborn's (5)
a) visual cortex is poorly developed
b) cone receptors are long and thin
c) cone receptors are short and widely spaced
d) a and c

16.3   An experiment described in the book indicates that one source of information that newborns make use of to recognize their mother's face is (8)
a) the mother's hairline
b) the configuration of the eyes and mouth
c) the mother's smell
d) the mother's smile

16.4   In an experiment by Quinn and coworkers, infants were habituated to vertical columns of squares, with one column being white squares, the next being black, and so on. They concluded that the infant's were able to perceptually group the black squares together and the white squares together, because the infants looked longer at a _____ grating when stimuli were changed from the squares to gratings (10)
a) vertical
b) horizontal

16.5   The principle that has enabled researchers to
        determine whether an infant has medium- and long-
        wavelength cones is (15)
        a) that the medium- and long-wavelength cones far
           outnumber the short-wavelength cones.
        b) infants tend to prefer greens and reds to blues
           when given a choice
        c) the short-wavelength cone is very poorly developed
           at birth
        d) Only the medium- and long-wavelength cones absorb
           light at wavelengths above 550 nm.

16.6   A stereogram would most likely be used to measure
        (20)
        a) binocular fixation
        b) the ability to see disparity information
        c) the ability to see forms
        d) visual acuity

16.7   Which type of depth perception develops first in
        infants? (22, 23)
        a) perception based on binocular disparity
        b) perception based on pictorial cues
        c) neither of the above. The use of both pictorial
           and disparity information develop at about the
           same rate

16.8   Infants can make smooth eye movements to follow a
        moving stimulus, by about _____ weeks of age (24)
        a) 2
        b) 6
        c) 12
        d) 24

16.9   Newborns can recognize their mother's voice (27)
        a) True
        b) False

16.10 The procedure that was used to show that newborns can hear and can localize sounds was (28)
a) habituation
b) head turning
c) preferential hearing
d) observer based psychoacoustic procedure

16.11 Newborn infants can recognize the odor of their mother's breast. (35)
a) True
b) False

16.12 The results of selective rearing experiments tell us that the development of adult perceptual abilities is (38)
a) due mainly to genetic programming
b) due mainly to perceptual experience while growing up
c) the result of an interaction between biological programming and perceptual experience
d) an inevitable outcome of biological forces that are generally beyond our control

16.13 Emmetropia refers to (40)
a) the process of development that results in the ability to perceive depth
b) the change in perception that occurs when an animal is raised in a strange environment
c) the development of abnormal vision (myopia or hyperopia) during early development
d) normal focusing of light onto the retina

16.14 In Kaye and Bower's experiment which showed that newborns can match a shape they feel to one they see, the shape was felt with the infant's (47)
a) hands
b) feet
c) mouth
d) cheek

CHAPTER 17

CLINICAL ASPECTS OF VISION AND HEARING
VISUAL IMPAIRMENT

Vision and hearing can be compromised by damage to a number of different structures in each system. This chapter documents the effects of damage to major structures in the visual and auditory systems and also describes what happens during vision and hearing examinations.

CHAPTER ORGANIZATION

1. How vision can become impaired.

2. What problems occur and how are they treated for (a) focusing problems; (b) decreased transmission of light (cornea and lens); (c) retinal damage, and (d) optic nerve damage (glaucoma).

3. What happens during an eye examination.

4. How hearing can become impaired.

5. What problems occur and how are they treated for (a) conductive hearing loss, and (b) sensorineural hearing loss.

6. What happens during a hearing examination.

7. How hearing loss is managed (if hearing can't be restored).

TABLE OF CONTENTS AND KEY TERMS

- retinoscopy exam
- external eye exam
- slit-lamp examination
- tonometry
- tonometer
- applanator
- ophthalmoscopy
- ophthalmoscope
- fluorescein angiography
- electroretinogram

Hearing Impairment

How Can Hearing Become Impaired? (535)
- hearing impairment
- hearing handicap

Conductive Hearing Loss (536)
- conductive hearing loss

Outer-Ear Disorders
Middle-Ear Disorders
- otitis media
- otosclerosis

Sensorineural Hearing Loss (537)
- sensorineural hearing loss

Presbycusis
- presbycusis

Noise-Induced Hearing Loss
- noise-induced hearing loss
- acoustic trauma

Tinnitus
- tinnitus
- tinnitus masker

Meniere's Disease
- Meniere's disease

Neural Hearing Loss

NOTES: CHAPTER 17

The two Tables below summarize information about disorders and treatment that are discussed in more detail in the book:

Table 17.1 Vision disorders and treatment.

Note: In general, treatment for most of these disorders begins with drug therapy. When that doesn't work, then surgical procedures are considered.

Problem	Site of Damage	Treatment
Corneal disease and injury (522)	Cornea	Corneal transplant
Cataract (523)	Lens	Removal of cataract and insertion of intraocular lens
Diabetic retinopathy (524)	Retinal circulation (neovascularization)	Laser photocoagulation Panretinal laser photo-coagulation Vitrectomy
Macular degeneration (526)	Cone receptors in macula (fovea) and retinal circulation (similar to diabetic retinopathy).	Laser photocoagulation (for selected patients).
Detached retina (526)	Retina (separated from pigment epithelium)	Surgery to reattach retina

Hereditary retinal degeneration (527)	Retina (example: retinitis pigmentosa)	None
Glaucoma (528)	Front of eyeball and optic nerve	Closed angle glaucoma: Iridectomy (hole in iris) Open angle glaucoma: Operation to open pathway through side of eyeball.

Table 17.2 Hearing disorders and treatment

Problem	Site/Description	Treatment
Outer ear disorder (536)	Blockage of outer ear canal	Surgery to remove blockage
Otitis media (536)	Middle ear infection	Drugs
Otosclerosis (537)	Growth of bones in middle ear so stapes becomes fixed	Stapedectomy. Replace stapes with artificial strut.
Presbycusis (537)	Hair cell damage	Amplification by hearing aid

Table 17.2 (Continued)

Problem	Site/Description	Treatment
Acoustic trauma (538)	Bones in middle ear or receptors in inner ear at receptors	No good treatment
Tinnitus (538)	Middle ear or inner ear	No good treatment. Tinnitus masker
Meniere's disease (538)	Buildup of liquid in cochlea and semi-circular canals	No one treatment available. Hearing aid
Neural hearing loss (539)	Tumor on the auditory nerve	Surgery to remove tumor

KEY TERMS: CHAPTER 17

Acoustic reflex. Activating of the middle ear muscles in response to high-intensity sounds.

Acoustic trauma. Damage to the inner ear caused by implosive noises such as those created by explosions or machines.

Age-related macular degeneration. Degeneration of the macular area of the retina associated with old age.

Applanator. The part of an applanation tonometer that is pushed against the patient's cornea to determine the intraocular pressure.

Articulation function. A plot of the number of words identified correctly versus the intensity of the words. Used to determine the presence of conductive or sensorineural hearing loss.

Astigmatism. A condition in which vision is blurred in some orientations because of a misshapen cornea.

Audiogram. A plot of the threshold for hearing pure tones versus the frequencies of the tones. Threshold in an audiogram is plotted relative to "normal threshold," which is set at "0," so normal hearing would be indicated by a horizontal line at "0" threshold.

Audiologist. A professional with a master's or doctoral degree who measures the hearing ability of children and adults to identify the presence and severity of any hearing problems. Audiologists also fit hearing-impaired people with hearing aids and teach them strategies for more effective communication.

Audiometer. A device for measuring an audiogram.

Aural rehabilitation. Training for hearing-impaired people that consists of training in speech reading and other communication strategies.

Axial myopia. See Myopia, axial.

Blindness. A visual acuity of 20/200 or less after correction or little peripheral vision (the legal definition of blindness).

Cataract, congenital. A cataract present at birth.

Cataract, secondary. A cataract caused by another eye disease.

Cataract, senile. A cataract due to old age. This is the most common form of cataract.

Cataract, traumatic. A cataract caused by injury.

Cataract. A lens that is clouded.

Cochlear implant. A device in which electrodes are inserted into the cochlea to create hearing by electrically stimulating the auditory nerve fibers. This device is used to restore hearing in people who have lost their hearing because of damaged hair cells.

Conductive hearing loss. Hearing loss that occurs when the vibrations of a sound stimulus are not conducted normally from the outer ear into the cochlea.

Congenital cataract. see Cataract, congenital.

Corneal disease and injury. Any disease or injury that damages the cornea, causing a loss of transparency.

Corneal transplant. The replacement of a damaged piece of cornea with a piece of healthy cornea taken from a donor.

Detached retina. A condition in which the retina is detached from the back of the eye.

Diabetes. A condition in which the body doesn't produce enough insulin. One side effect of diabetes is a loss of vision due to diabetic retinopathy.

Diabetic retinopathy. Damage to the retina that is a side effect of diabetes. This condition causes neovascularization--the formation of abnormal blood vessels that do not supply the retina with adequate oxygen and that bleed into the vitreous humor.

Diopter. The strength of a lens. Diopters = 1/far point in meters.

Electroretinogram. An electrical response of the visual receptors that is used in diagnosing retinal degenerations.

External eye exam. Examination of the condition of the outer eye. This exam includes, among other things, examination of the reaction of the pupil to light, the color of the eye, and the alignment of the eyes.

Far point. The distance at which the rays from a spot of light are focused on the retina of the unaccommodated eye. For a person with normal vision, the far point is at infinity. For a person with myopic vision, the spot must be moved closer to the eye to bring the rays to a focus on the retina.

Farsightedness. See Hyperopia.

Fluorescein angiography. A technique in which a fluorescent dye is injected into a person's circulation. The outline of the retinal arteries and veins produced by this dye gives information about the condition of the retinal circulation.

Glaucoma, closed-angle. A rare form of glaucoma in which the iris is pushed up so that it closes the angle between the iris and the cornea and blocks the area through which the aqueous humor normally drains out of the eye.

Glaucoma, open-angle. A form of glaucoma in which the area through which the aqueous humor normally drains out of the eye is blocked. In this form of glaucoma, the iris remains in its normal position so that the angle between the iris and the cornea remains open.

Glaucoma. A disease of the eye that usually results in an increase in intraocular pressure.

Hearing handicap. The disadvantage that a hearing impairment causes in a person's ability to communicate or in the person's daily living.

Hearing impairment. A deviation or change for the worse in either the structure or the functioning of the auditory system (see Hearing handicap).

Hereditary retinal degeneration. A degeneration of the retina that is inherited. Retinitis pigmentosa is an example of a hereditary retinal degeneration.

Hyperopia (farsightedness). The inability to see near objects clearly because the focus point for parallel rays of light is behind the retina.

Intraocular lens. A plastic or silicone lens that is inserted into the eye after the removal of a cataract. This lens partially compensates for the loss of focusing power caused by removal of the patient's lens.

Intraocular pressure. Pressure inside the eyeball.

Iridectomy. A procedure used to treat closed-angle glaucoma, in which a small hole is cut in the iris. This hole opens a channel through which aqueous humor can flow out of the eye.

Laser photocoagulation. A procedure in which a laser beam is aimed at blood vessels that are leaking because of neovascularization. This laser beam photocoagulates--seals off--the blood vessels and stops the leaking.

Laser photorefractive keratotomy. A surgical procedure in which an excimer laser is used to change the shape of the cornea to improve the vision of people with myopia or hyperopia.

Macula. An area about 5 mm in diameter, that surrounds and includes the fovea.

Macular degeneration, age related. The most common form of macular degeneration, occurring in older people.

Macular degeneration. A degeneration of the macula area of the retina.

Meniere's disease. A form of sensorineural hearing loss caused by an excessive buildup of the liquid that fills the cochlea and the semicircular canals.

Myopia (nearsightedness). The inability to see distant objects clearly because parallel rays of light are brought to a focus in front of the retina.

Myopia, axial. Myopia caused by an elongated eyeball.

Myopia, refractive. Myopia that occurs when the cornea and the lens bend light too much (they have too much focusing power).

Neovascularization. The formation of abnormal small blood vessels that occurs in patients with diabetic retinopathy.

Noise-induced hearing loss. A form of sensorineural hearing loss that occurs when loud noises cause degeneration of the hair cells.

Ophthalmologist. A person who has specialized in the medical treatment of the eye by completing four or more years of training after receiving the M. D. degree.

Ophthalmoscope. A device that enables an examiner to see the retina and the retinal circulation inside the eye.

Ophthalmoscopy. The use of an ophthalmoscope to visualize the retina and the retinal circulation.

Optician. A person who is trained to fit glasses and, in some cases, contact lenses.

Optometrist. A person who has received the doctor of optometry (O. D.) degree by completing four years of postgraduate study in optometry school.

Otitis media. An infection of the middle ear.

Otologist. An otorhinolaryngologist whose practice is limited to problems involving the auditory and vestibular systems.

Otorhinolaryngologist. A medical doctor who has specialized in the treatment of diseases and disorders affecting the ear, nose, and throat. More commonly known as an ENT (ear, nose, and throat) specialist.

Otosclerosis. A hereditary condition in which there is a growth of bone in the middle ear.

Otoscope. A device used to see the tympanic membrane.

Panretinal photocoagulation. A procedure in which a laser is used to create many small burns on the retina. This procedure has been successful in treating the neovascularization associated with diabetic retinopathy.

Phacoemulsification. A technique for removing a cataract by breaking up the lens with ultrasonic vibrations and then sucking the pieces of lens out of the eye through a hollow needle.

Presbycusis. A form of sensorineural hearing loss that occurs as a function of age and is usually associated with a decrease in the ability to hear high frequencies. Since this loss also appears to be related to exposure to environmental sounds, it is also called sociocusis.

Presbyopia ("old eye"). The inability of the eye to accommodate due to the hardening of the lens and a weakening of the ciliary muscles. It occurs as people get older.

Pupillary block. A blockage that constricts the opening between the iris and the lens of the eye, making it difficult for aqueous humor to leave the eye. It is caused by the pushed-up iris characteristic of closed-angle glaucoma.

Pure-tone audiometry. Measurement of the threshold for hearing as a function of the frequency of a pure tone.

Radial keratotomy. A surgical procedure in which four to eight cuts are placed radially around the cornea. When successful, this operation decreases the focusing power of the cornea and improves the vision of people with myopia.

Refraction. A procedure used to determine the power of the corrective lenses needed to achieve clear vision.

Refractive myopia. See Myopia, refractive.

Retinitis pigmentosa. A retinal disease that causes a gradual loss of vision.

Retinoscopy exam. Examination with a device called a retinoscope that indicates the power of the corrective lenses needed to achieve normal vision.

Secondary cataract. see Cataract, secondary.

Senile cataract. see Cataract, senile.

Slit lamp examination. An examination that checks the condition of the cornea and lens.

Tinnitus masker. A unit that generates white noise to mask the ringing in the ears associated with tinnitus.

Tinnitus. A condition caused by damage in the inner ear in which a person experiences ringing in the ears.

Tonometer. A device for measuring the eye's intraocular pressure.

Tonometry. An examination that determines the pressure inside the eye.

Tunnel vision. Vision that results when there is little peripheral vision.

Tympanometer. A device for measuring how well the tympanic membrane and the middle-ear bones respond to sound vibrations.

Tympanometry. Procedure for measuring how well the tympanic membrane and middle ear bones are responding to sound vibrations.

Visual perimetry. A procedure for testing vision that tests a person's ability to detect small spot stimuli presented at various locations in the person's visual field.

Vitrectomy. A procedure in which a needle placed inside the eye removes vitreous humor and replaces it with a salt solution. This procedure is used if the vitreous humor is filled with blood, usually because of neovascularization.

Vitreous humor. The jelly like substance that fills the eyeball.

TEST YOURSELF

Indicate which eye problems occur at the sites indicated.
See Figure 17.2 to check your answer.

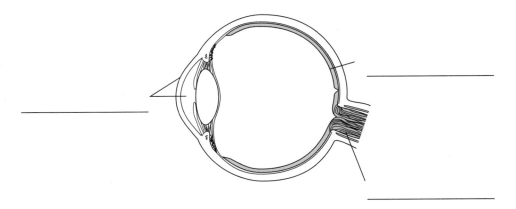

Indicate which hearing problems occur at the sites
indicated. See Figure 17.28 to check your answer.

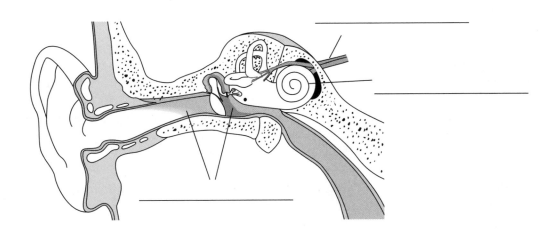

MULTIPLE CHOICE QUESTIONS

17.1 Myopia can be caused by (2)
a) a lens that is too weak
b) a lens that is too powerful
c) a misshapen (not symmetrical) cornea
d) none of the above

17.2 Eye operations that cause the cornea to become flatter, cause the focus point to move _____ the front of the eye (7)
a) toward
b) away from

17.3 A hyperope's focus point is _____ the retina for far away objects. (8)
a) in front of
b) behind

17.4 Which of the following is an example of a problem that occurs because light is blurred when it enters the eye? (15)
a) cataract
b) myopia
c) glaucoma
d) presbyopia

17.5 Which of the following is not associated with diabetic retinopathy? (19)
a) neovascularization
b) photocoagulation
c) swelling capillaries
d) none of the above (they are all associated with diabetic retinopathy)

17.6 A procedure used to stop neovascularization is (20)
a) vitrectomy
b) laser photocoagulation
c) drug treatments
d) ophthalmoscopy

255

17.7   Detachment of the retina from the pigment epithelium
        causes (23)
        a) retinal bleeding
        b) a decrease in visual pigment regeneration
        c) a loss of central, but not peripheral, vision
        d) a degeneration of the pigment epithelium

17.8   The purpose of the slit lamp examination is to (33)
        a) check the condition of the retinal circulation
        b) precisely determine the ability to resolve small
           details
        c) determine the condition of the lens and cornea
        d) examine the structures in the outer ear

17.9   Tonometry is used to determine (34)
        a) intraocular pressure
        b) the condition of the cornea and lens
        c) the condition of the pupil
        d) the shape of the eyeball

17.10   A crucial component of an ophthalmoscope is (35)
        a) a small plunger that is pushed against the eyeball
           to measure the intraocular pressure
        b) a highly sensitive photocell that measures the
           intensity of light reflected out of the eyeball
        c) directing light into the patient's eye using a
           half-silvered mirror
        d) an ultra low intensity laser beam that illuminates
           the retina

17.11   Swelling of the ear canal would cause a _____
        hearing loss.(40)
        a) sensorineural
        b) conductive

17.12   Tinnitus (45)
        a) is a loss of hearing at high frequencies
        b) can be permanently eliminated by wearing a
           tinnitus masker for about a week
        c) is a slight ringing in the ears which can be
           easily ignored
        d) cannot be cured

17.13 The articulation function is part of a test of (52)
    a) the ability to produce words accurately
    b) sound transmission through the auditory system
    c) word recognition
    d) the thresholds for hearing tones that are located
       within the frequency range for speech perception

17.14 When blind people have had vision restored, the
       outcome has not always been positive because (57)
    a) their vision has often regressed back into
       blindness
    b) they can "see" light, but are not able to actually
       perceive objects
    c) the people have suffered from depression after the
       operation
    d) they have then lost the enhanced senses of touch
       and hearing that developed when they were blind

17.15 In an experiment described in the text, it was found
       that people who are deaf scored _____ than hearing
       subjects on a test of visual attention. (58, 59)
    a) higher
    b) lower

APPENDIX

SIGNAL DETECTION THEORY

TABLE OF CONTENTS AND KEY TERMS

KEY TERMS: APPENDIX

Correct rejection In a signal detection experiment, saying, "No, I don't detect a stimulus" on a trial in which the stimulus is not presented (a correct response).

False alarm. In a signal detection experiment, saying, "Yes, I detect the stimulus" on a trial in which the stimulus is not presented (an incorrect response).

Hit. In a signal detection experiment, saying, "Yes, I detect a stimulus" on a trial in which the stimulus is present (a correct response).

Miss. In a signal detection experiment, saying, "No, I don't detect a stimulus" on a trial in which the stimulus is present (an incorrect response).

Noise. All stimuli in the environment other than the signal. Noise can also be generated within a person's nervous system. The subject's perception of noise in a signal detection experiment sometimescauses the subject to think mistakenly that a signal has been presented.

Payoffs. A system of rewards and punishments used to influence a subject's motivation in a signal detection experiment.

Receiver operating characteristic (ROC curve). A graph in which the results of a signal detection experiment are plotted as the proportion of hits versus the proportion of false alarms for a number of different response criteria.

Response criterion. In a signal detection experiment, the subjective magnitude of a stimulus above which the subject will indicate that the stimulus is present. (Appendix)

Signal. The stimulus presented to a subject. A concept in signal detection theory

Signal detection theory. A theory stating that the detection of a stimulus depends both on the subject's sensitivity to the stimulus and on the subject's response criterion.

TEST YOURSELF

MULTIPLE CHOICE QUESTIONS

A.1 An observer is told that on each trial she is to describe whether or not she sees a flash of light. On one of the trials no light flash is presented but she says "yes" (she thinks she saw a flash of light). This response is a (a)
a) false alarm
b) hit
c) miss
d) correct rejection

A.2 A signal detection experiment is run using the following payoffs: Hit: Win $10; Correct rejection: Win $100; False alarm: Lose $10; Miss: Lose $10. These payoffs result in (c)
a) an increase in the subject's threshold
b) a decrease in the subject's threshold
c) an increase in the subject's criterion
d) a decrease in the subject's criterion

A.3 Increased sensitivity (c)
a) has no effect on the probability distributions for N and S + N
b) decreases the distance between the probability distributions
c) increases the distance between the probability distributions

ANSWERS TO MULTIPLE-CHOICE QUESTIONS

Chapter 1

1	d
2	c
3	c
4	b
5	c
6	c
7	d
8	b
9	d
10	a
11	b
12	b

Chapter 2

1	c
2	a
3	a
4	b
5	a
6	d
7	c
8	a
9	a
10	c
11	b
12	c
13	a
14	b
15	a
16	b
17	c
18	b
19	c

Chapter 3

1	a
2	a
3	a
4	b
5	d
6	a
7	d
8	c
9	d
10	a
11	b
12	d
13	c
14	c
15	a
16	a
17	b

Chapter 4

1	b
2	a
3	b
4	a
5	c
6	b
7	b
8	a
9	b
10	b
11	a
12	b

Chapter 5

1	c
2	d
3	a
4	a
5	b
6	b
7	d
8	b
9	b
10	a
11	d
12	c
13	b
14	c
15	b
16	b

Chapter 6

1	b
2	c
3	a
4	d
5	b
6	b
7	a
8	c

Chapter 7

1	b
2	a
3	d
4	a
5	d
6	a
7	b
8	c
9	b
10	a
11	a
12	d
13	a
14	b
15	a

Chapter 8

1	b
2	a
3	c
4	b
5	b
6	c
7	a
8	d
9	c
10	a
11	b
12	b
13	b
14	d
15	c

Chapter 9

1	b
2	d
3	d
4	c
5	b
6	d
7	c
8	a
9	b
10	d
11	c
12	a
13	d
14	b
15	d

Chapter 10

1	d
2	d
3	b
4	a
5	d
6	a
7	b
8	c
9	a
10	c
11	b
12	b
13	c
14	d
15	a

Chapter 11

1	a
2	c
3	b
4	d
5	b
6	c
7	a
8	a
9	b
10	b
11	a
12	c
13	b
14	c
15	d

Chapter 12

1	c
2	b
3	a
4	a
5	c
6	b
7	a

8	c
9	b
10	c
11	a
12	b
13	a
14	b
15	c

Chapter 13

1	b
2	a
3	c
4	b
5	c
6	b
7	b
8	d
9	c
10	a
11	b
12	a
13	d
14	c
15	d

Chapter 14

1	c
2	c
3	c
4	d
5	a
6	d
7	a
8	c
9	b
10	d
11	a
12	d
13	d
14	c

Chapter 15

1	a
2	c
3	a
4	c
5	b
6	b
7	c
8	d
9	a
10	d
11	a
12	b
13	b
14	a
15	c

Chapter 16

1	c
2	d
3	a
4	b
5	d
6	b
7	b
8	c
9	a
10	b
11	a
12	c
13	d
14	c

Chapter 17

1	b
2	b
3	a
4	a
5	d
6	b
7	b
8	c
9	a
10	b
11	b
12	d
13	c
14	c
15	b

Appendix

1	a
2	c
3	c